Guardians of the Forest

Smithsonian's National Museum of the American Indian in New York, the George Gustav Heye Center

April 22th - September 21st, 2008

REVISITED

Expanded version - all images taken between 2003 - 2008

Credits

Simithsonian's National Museum of the American Indian in New York
The George Gustav Heye Center

Director
John Haworth

Deputy Director of Exhibitions and Programs
Petre Brill

Latin American Media Coordinator
Amalia Cordova

Public Affairs Associate
Quinn Bradley

Manager of Education
Johanna Gorelick

Exhibition Associate
Robert Mastrangelo

Events Manager
Trey Moynihan

Exhibition Specialist
John Richardson

Program Producer
Shawn Termin

Public Affairs Office
Ann Marie Sekeres

Events Associate
Melissa Vasquez

Head of Film + Video Center
Elizabeth Weatherford

Exhibition

Brazilian Organizers
Fare Arte & Amazonia Brasil

Internacional Production & Coordination
Alvisse Migotto

Catalogue

Texts
John Haworth / Amador Grinó Andrés

Photographs
Rodrigo Petrella

Interview
Daniel Dinato

Traslations
English - Amanda Nolen / Melanie Wyffels

Guardians of the Forest
& The Mapinguary

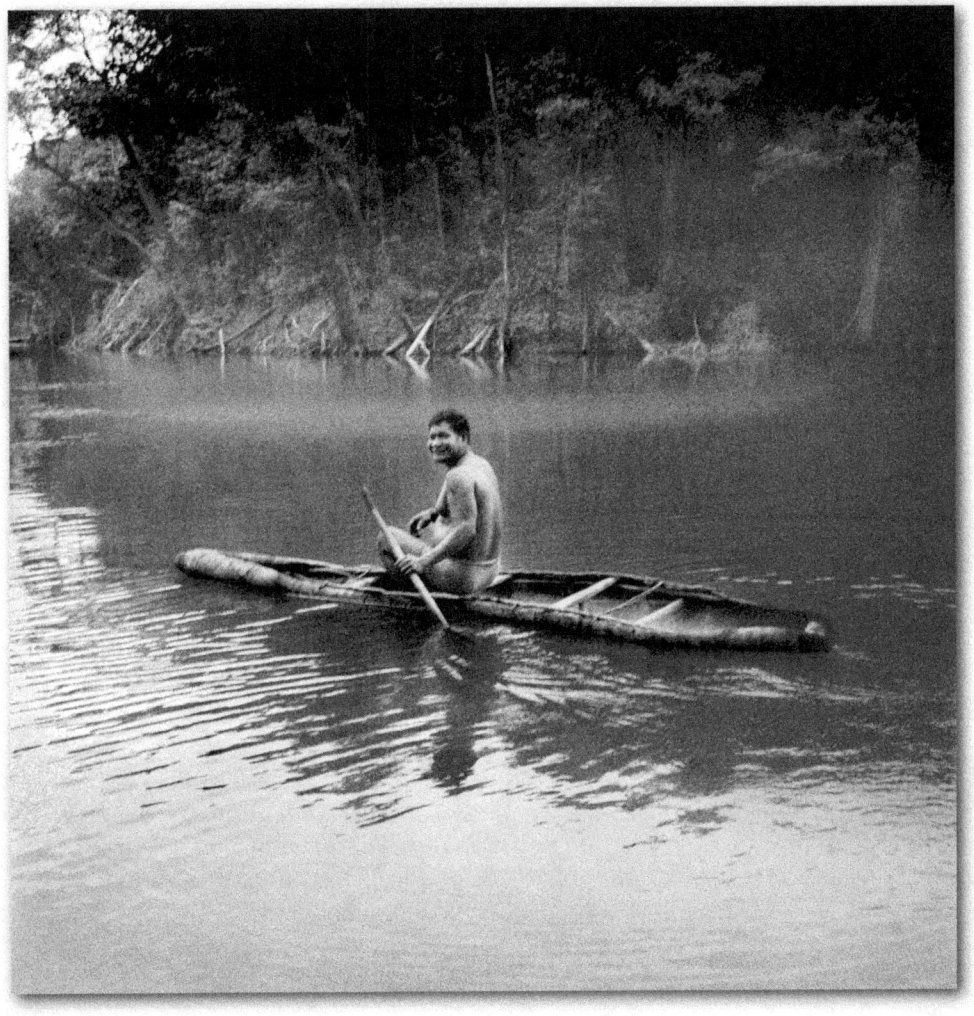

Pirahã / skin-tree canoe at the igapós of Repartimento T.I. Parintintin

Forest Revisited

FOREWORDS & INTERVIEW BY DANIEL DINATO

A little more than a decade after my first solo exhibition, I feel the need —a therapeutic need, I would say— to revisit this experience. With this experience I was exposed to an art system which, from that moment on, would determine to a large extent the paths that I would take in my life. However, as it all occurred in the midst of a vertiginous sequence of political events in the Amazon, deeply rooted in local issues and somehow unrelated to the big political and economic changes on a global scale, perhaps the distance in time might now help me to better understand it.

It might help me understand not only my personal processes on this journey, my choices and my resignations, whether they were conscious or not, but also the stories and narratives I have told, to understand the way these stories are legitimate and how they are validated by other accounts. Above all, it may help me to understand the enormous changes which have been occurring in what may be described as the cultural ethos that these traditional peoples socially occupy. At this present moment, there is a liquid cartography of values, beliefs and feelings now strongly influenced and captured by social media and digital systems of identification which have deeply changed the functioning balance of this identitarian mechanism. Something that would be described better in simpler images, such as the moves of a pendulum that swings both towards the new and the traditional.

Last but not least, there is the global resurgence of hate speech towards difference, openly sectarian and racist. Regarding the Amazon tribes, once more their lands are the object of others' greed. Mining and oil companies, the logging industry, hydroelectric power projects and Christian missions, as well as the threat of industrial monoculture, and a move towards agricultural Fordism all threaten traditional modes of subsistence, and to irrevocably alter the unique ethnic-cultural character of these tribes. Will the indigenous people resist these processes that threaten the integrity of their respective cultures, and even their very existence?

****

Daniel: Rodrigo, could you tell us how this project began?

R: In 2007, when I had already been close to COIAB (Coordenação das Organizações Indígenas da Amazônia Brasileira, Coordination of the Indigenous Organizations of the Brazilian Amazon) for some time, I thought of bringing an idea to the internal debates. The image of indigenous peoples had a positive value, a substantial moral aspect that could serve the movement's political interests. In their case, it meant using what they defined as art — photography— as a mediation tool between the indigenous movement and the society. The idea was clear to Jecinaldo Sateré Mawé, COIAB executive coordinator back then.

After internal deliberation with other regional leaders and both national and international supporters, it was decided that a campaign should be organized in support of this aim. At the time we didn't know exactly what to do, but we knew that we had a powerful tool at our disposal. We thought of doing something with a certain educational aspect, in order to bring into view a little of this ethnic-cultural wealth, as well as bringing to wider public attention the immense challenges these people were facing, creating an invitation for conversation between these cultures and worlds —and with that which we conventionally call ours.

We chose some key issues regarding the Brazilian indigenous movement in 2007, such as the construction of Belo Monte power station. A threat to the

Xingu River, with its dams controlling the water flows, the project was beginning to take shape, and the environmental impact would reach and affect many riverside communities and indigenous ethnicities like the Kayapó, not to mention the plethora of SHP (Small Hydro Power) stations projects expected to be built in the same hydrographic basin, directly affecting the Xingu National Park and its people. Hydro power stations were —and are still— a serious issue looming on the horizon.

Also, I felt an emotional debt towards the north Nambikwara (Maimandê and Nambikwara do Campo), perhaps the first indigenous group to host me, especially towards the old chief Lourenço. I wanted them to feature in the project, but there weren't many dams where they lived, since southern Rondônia is a mountainous landscape. However, this kind of story of developments that directly and negatively impact upon traditional cultures and modes of subsistence is recurrent to many communities. In their case, they suffered with the construction of BR 364 road and the migratory flow that accompanied this, during the 1970s and 1980s. Caused by many tax incentives, it generated a disorderly occupation of the land and an economy based at first on activities such as logging, illegal mining and extensive farming. More recently, the cultivation of large-scale commodity crops has brought even more people to the region. That's when we decided to include the Nambikwara and some other groups.

In 2007, I was at a multi-stakeholder meeting about sustainability in Belém, Pará, with an indigenous delegation when I met a culture producer that was organizing a big event in New York. I was invited to present my work to the director and curator of the (1) Smithsonian National Museum of the American Indian, so that we could make parallel exhibitions. We didn't even realize that at the same time the UN would host the 7th session of the United Nations Permanent Forum on Indigenous Issues, which was a happy coincidence.

D: So, it was a project mediated by photography against the power station dams.

R: To some extent, yes, and also, a project that tried to expose the complexities of the indigenous world in Brazil to the outside world.

D: And the pictures were all yours?

R: Yes, they were all mine! It was a volunteer work, produced jointly by myself and by all those involved. I spent months working on this project, travelling and going everywhere in order to visit many communities and ethnicities with the help of COIAB. That was when I met the Mebêngrôke (2) (Gorotirê, Kriny village) and the Mehináku (3) (Kuikuro, Ypatse village). I photographed these people in a kind of traditional celebration and then, their leaders meeting against Belo Monte, so as to unite against this threat and raise awareness and publicity about the numerous mineral projects and dams expected to be built in the Amazon, projects that come with poisonous effects. Our hope was to create a debate about the projects that were expected to spread to other hydrographic basins such as Tapajós, Madeira, Purus...

Speaking of dams, that was what I had in mind when I photographed the Enawenê-Nawê (4) from a contrasting perspective, with their own temporary dams for fishing purposes, made of wood, stones and vines - a beautiful parallel when compared with our gigantic, monstrous dams. Finally, I visited the Yanomami (5), because the COIAB thought it was important to do so. "Go visit the Yanomami. Davi (6) is the man. Let's see how it goes," they said. That is what we did in 2007 —we travelled, talked and debated, collecting material to finally organize an exhibition (7) or something that would bring attention to the movement.

In the beginning of 2008, there was a change of plans brought about by a COIAB meeting at a farm near Manaus. The aim of the meeting was to decide which political strategies the movement representatives would follow during a UN plenary meeting in New York. As previously agreed, during the meeting we discussed the terms of COIAB's participation at the Smithsonian, as a result of their invitation. After internal deliberation the participation was approved under certain terms. The idea, which had at first been imagined as a big campaign, had finally developed to become embodied by this exhibition. I was there with the indigenous leaders, and they approved it. We had a partnership, a voluntary partnership. I was loyal to it and, after deliberating, I followed some of the content instructions they thought were the most important. It was suggested that we showed the peoples' diversity, with a bigger variety of ethnicities, focusing on children, as they thought the indigenous children were at risk. I didn't think that was the most interesting structure or idea, but, in a certain way, I could see that it was the manifestation of what they considered as a pertinent representation. The image editing was inspired by these suggestions...

D: And how was the exhibition?

R: On the opening day many indigenous leaders came. I had invited them on that same day, since they were already scheduled to be participating in the events at the UN, which resulted in a Fellini-like scene. It all happened spontaneously at NMAI, the National Museum of the American Indian — situated in the heart of Manhattan at the old Custom House building, where at one time, immigrants arriving in "America" had historically arrived. The leaders arrived and crossed a big hall towards the space where the photographs were exhibited. Behind them, in another room, were objects from the indigenous peoples of the US northwestern region, who used to make those wooden columns we conventionally call totems, although that is not what they actually are, objects created by peoples from Oregon and the Vancouver River region with names that I cannot pronounce (8). You see their objects and their sculptures, artifacts of peoples that were completely devastated by colonization, locked inside glass displays like relics of these civilizations —and then they come, Brazilian indigenous leaders crossing the rooms, dressed in their own cultures, with headdresses and ornaments, walking amidst those displays full of masks made of animal skin and wood...

D: Were Almir (Suruí) and Sonia (Guajajara) there?

R: Yes, they were there with other leaders, opening the exhibition on Earth Day, April 22nd. Almir made a very sensitive speech in defense of the indigenous peoples and their lands. It was very spontaneous, very beautiful, I was really touched. I remember just a few words, but I remember the lasting impression that the speech left me with... Today, more then 10 years later it still touches me. On the opening day, it was very hard to bring them from the UN to the museum, so they could attend both of the events... I remember the institution directors and anthropologists and the other invited people were all visibly touched by their presence. It was beautiful!

1 Smithsonian refers to the National Museum of the American Indian (NMAI), an anthropology museum which is a branch of the Smithsonian Institute. The NMAI owns pieces and artefacts of indigenous peoples from the American continent, from Tierra del Fuego to the Artic Circle. For other information visit http://nmai.si.edu.

2 Mebêngrôke, meaning the "people from the water hole", is the name the Kayapó call themselves. They live in the states of Pará and Matogrosso. Their population is around 8 thousand people divided into seven groups —Gorotire, Kuben-Krân-Krên, Kôkraimôrô, Kararaô, Mekrãgnoti, Metyktire and Xikrin.

3 The Mehináku, speakers of an Aruak language, are comprised of approximately 300 people living by the margins of Curievo River, in the region of High Xingu, Mato Grosso state.

4 The Enawenê-Nawê live in a single village named Halataikwa. They are comprised of approximately 700 people divided into 10 clans, which count amongst their ranks not only people, but also subterranean and celestial spirits related to flute groups and descendants of mythical populations that came out of stones and spread through the region. They speak an Aruak language and live in the northwest region of Matogrosso state.

5 The Yanomami are 25 thousand people living in the northern region of the Amazon between Brazil and Venezuela. They are speakers of a Yanomami language which constitute a cultural group with at least four subdivisions Yanomae, Yanõmami, Sanima and Ninam.

6 Davi Kopenawa Yanomami is one of the main indigenous leaders not only in Brazil but also globally. He is a shaman and a leader. Recently, he published the book "The Falling Sky" with anthropologist Bruce Albert. The book is a cosmo-political tractate that brings Davi's words and views to our non-indigenous world.

7 Before the exhibition at the NMAI, the COIAB photographs were initially to have been exhibited at the Global Bank, Washington D.C. This exhibition ultimately did not happen in quite the way it had been planned and thus was moved to Brasília. It was during this process that the NMAI made the invitation and new negotiations had to be handled with the COIAB.

8 This is a reference to the Kwakwaka'wakw, an indigenous group of 3500 people living in the region of British Columbia.

Guardians of the Forest

GUARDIANS OF THE FOREST

Looking carefully at photographs is a way for us viewers to develop a deeper understanding of a-far-away place beyond our own direct experience and individual worldviews, In 2008, the National Museum of the American Indian's George Gustav Heye Center in New York City presented the exhibition "Guardians of the Forest" by the well-known Sao Paulo photographer Rodrigo Petrella. Having established a strong reputation 'as a highly regarded artist' working in the fields of ant and fashion photography in New York City, in the aftermath of 9/11, Petrella returned to Brazil and began working on a comprehensive socially-committed project in the Amazon taking photographs of the indigenous people of the Brazilian Amazon. From his massive body of work, including scores of images of daily and communal life within this complex and biologically diverse environment, my museum worked with Petrella to develop this extensive exhibition.

"Guardians" was part of a series of educational programs focusing on climate change, economic sustainability, and indigenous leadership and interactive exhibitions at three lower Manhattan venues: the South Street Seaport's 'Pier 17 which housed a 13,000-square-foot recreation of the Amazon, the World Financial Center and the National Museum of the American Indian.

The Brazilian-based organization Amazônia Brasil, created to raise awareness about the diverse ecosystems of the Brazilian Amazon rainforest, took the leadership role in developing and presenting these wonderful programs. Serendipitously, in spring 2008, my museum's Film + Video Center presented a complementary media program, a retrospective of award-winning video

productions by indigenous video-makers from the Brazilian Amazon through "
Video Amazônia Indígena: A View from the Villages "

Photographers used to posing and 'capturing' fashionable images run the risk of
voyeurism, that is, objectifying or glamorizing human beings, rather than
presenting nuanced images that communicate deeper meanings to the viewer.
Indeed, Petrella's photographs are beautifully rendered revealing a level of
technical accomplishment and polish, and yet, he works on a far more
substantive level grounded in respect to reveal subtleties about the social,
economic and physical environment of the indigenous people we see in the
finished images. Viewing his Amazonian images, it is clear that Petrella
developed a thorough understanding and respect both of the lives of the people
he photographed and the communities that sustained their lives. It also was to
clear to me that he earned the respect of the indigenous communities
themselves, allowing him to be initiated into their communities to hear their
stories and tell them to us through photographic images. Seeing his work
encourages all of us to learn more about this remarkable region and to examine
its myriad of meanings.This is the spirit of his work.

For the National Museum of the American Indian, a cultural institution
grounded in bringing forth a First Person perspective in all that we do, our
primary focus is showing work in all media, including photography, made by
Native people themselves.

When Amazonia Brasil proposed that the NMAI, as one of their New York-based
collaborative partners, develop an exhibit of Petralla's work, we expressed our
initial concerns about presenting Petrella's work, mainly because we thought it
may have lacked the active participation of community-based indigenous
people of this region. Far too often, we have seen images which enforce negative
stereotypes of Native people as "Noble Savages" or romanticized images that
present images of indigenous people as being Long Gone. We had tremendous
confidence, however, in the spirited and community-based work of our
collaborator Amazônia Brasil. Created by the Projeto Saúde e Alegria (Health
and Happiness Project), Amazônia Brasil is the culmination of extensive

research and collaborations with more than 600 organizations. In the early stages of developing "Guardians," it became absolutely clear that Petrella had developed a close working relationship with the Amazon-based indigenous communities and that his commitment was Both culturally sensitive and deep. "Guardians" calls attention to the COIAB, the Coordination of the Indigenous Organizations of the Brazilian Amazon, which happens to be the most representative association of indigenous peoples from the Amazon.

Over the last few years especially, NMAI itself has developed a far deeper understanding of the importance of incorporating information in our exhibitions and public programs that are both informed by an indigenous perspective and giving attention to environmental concerns. Indeed, green is the color of the moment. Everywhere from the grocery store, the office and yes, even museums - there are newer and trendier reminders urging us to protect the precious resources of the earth. "Guardians" certainly brought focused attention to the importance of environment stewardship and gave us greater insights about sustaining the' environment. These images make us consider the importance of the Amazon to everyone everywhere on our planet, and help us understand that this region must be honored and preserved. Seeing rich documentation of this region gives us powerful evidence about how indigenous people are connected to where they live and how their lives are shaped by this complex environment and vice versa. It is critically important that significantly more people outside the Amazon become keenly aware of and understand more fully the social, political and economic dynamics at play.

Traditionally, images of Native people are often used to illustrate responsible land use, conservation, and ecology. Remember the old 1970's "Keep America Beautiful" commercial with Iron Eyes Cody? Trash scatters at the feet of Cody, who turns to the camera and sheds a single tear. But what does it really mean when N native people actively protect the land?

Native lands comprise over 20% of the Amazon Basin, one of the planet's most important resources. In Brazil, indigenous lands belong to the government but Native people have usage rights in perpetuity. Because of threats from loggers, miners and poachers, indigenous lands are often the only areas of preserved forest and serve as a real means of protection to the unbelievable diversity and wealth of the region- including tens of thousands plant and animal species, 23 ecosystems, and 20 billion tons of water vapor produced daily that regulates the word's climate.

For well over a decade, in my capacity as Director of the National Museum of the American Indian's George Gustav HeyeCenter in New York City, I have had the opportunity of working on many worthwhile public programs and exhibitions about the indigenous arts and cultures of the Americas. In fall 2007, two lower Manhattan colleagues and I traveled to the Rio Tapajos region in the Amazon with a group of Brazilian researchers, doctors, cultural activists and producers on a trip organized by Amazônia Brasil. I had the privilege of meeting with Native people throughout this region and witnessed first-hand the incredible commitment made by their communities to protecting the land and experience vivid demonstrations of their active stewardship. While there are Brazilian and international organizations providing assistance in the fields of medicine, education, and technology, the indigenous communities themselves play the primary role in protecting their forests and developing their local economies through collaborative and sustainable initiatives. Most certainly, the indigenous people of the Amazon are the primary caretakers the Guardians of the Forest which is also their homeland.

Sadly, I also saw massive areas where the forest had been cleared to make way for aggressive agricultural development. The external and financial pressures are enormously complicated but the consequences of these acts impact all of us, everywhere. I continue to be inspired by the strength of the Native people of the Amazon - despite their enormous challenges, they continue to preserve their heritages and move forward into the future. Hearing the local perspective from a deeply informed account of how traditional people are forced off their lands resulting in the loss of their communities and spirits in the name of economic development, "progress" and globalization was incredibly sad and depressing. Being in the Amazon with Amazônia Brasil colleagues - some of the most dedicated, hopeful and tireless people I've ever encountered - was an incredibly *affirming and transformative experience.*

The photographs shown in this exhibition evidence the presence and diversity of the Native people of the Amazon. According to Amazônia Brasil, more than 440,000 indigenous people who hail from an estimated 220 ethnic groups and speak 160 languages live in the Brazilian Amazon. These photographs by Rodrigo Petrella offer a glimpse into the rich lives and complex cultures of indigenous people who have lived harmoniously with nature for centuries and offer vital insight into how the future of the planet can be sustained.

John Haworth (Cherokee)

Director, the George Gustav Heye Center

National Museum of the American Indian, New York City

The Mapinguarí

THE MAPINGUARI

The Indians believe that in the State of Acre, in the Amazon River basin, there lives a being two meters in height covered with red hair. It resembles a man, but has just a single eye in the middle of its forehead like the mythological Cyclops, and across its stomach is a huge mouth which it uses to devour unfortunate souls who venture into the jungle and cross its path.

There was a time when a lack of information, coupled with fear - that powerful guardian of inscrutable secrets - was a weapon used to protect treasures and possessions. People did not dare to enter haunted houses, numerous tombs prevented grave robbers from looting their contents, for fear of being cursed. Likewise, the belief that forests and jungles were guarded by unspeakable dangers - strange beasts and fantastic creatures postponed the destructive, consumerist spiral of rampant development.

That atavistic fear that the wet, primeval jungle - an imaginary reflection of the lost garden of paradise and original creation - once held over the Western subconscious no longer has the power to inhibit us. Now, the secrecy and lack of information that once surrounded it have become the best ally of logging companies, unscrupulous mineral mining, agriculture and livestock production.

The people who inhabit this jungle, the erroneously-named Indians - unable to stop the growing exploitation of their ancestral home, unable to fight the global market's need for raw materials are exterminated in ways crueler than immediate death (which is also common). And so, they are murdered a thousand times over, in a thousand different ways, with each passing day and on every acre that is burned and deforested.

Stripped of their identity, origins and culture, they are nothing. We condemn them to become little more than animals who can speak. By acting as if they didn't exist, we avoid feelings of guilt and make it easier to eliminate them. What is not publicized does not exist, as any researcher will tell you. If there are no inhabitants, all that is left is forest brush covering up the riches that lie under the ground. Responsibility is thus limited to a bad environmental conscience, which can be alleviated through projects for the selective, programmed felling of trees, reforestation and lowering pollution.

Rodrigo Petrella, with his cycloid, mechanical eye, like a new kind of Mapinguarí, offers us an admirable, realistic vision of its inhabitants. His photographs, without any documentary or anthropological pretensions, show us a universe that exists in parallel to our own reality.

It is his passion for photography that led him to penetrate the jungle. He chose the Amazon for obvious cultural reasons and for its geographical proximity. His vision - his photographs - show Amazonian Indians who are nothing like the stereotypical 19th-century "good savage", and force us to face everyday indigenous existence at the crossroads it finds itself at, that non-reality trapped between two worlds.

This new reality which photography creates by capturing it on paper, this dimension constructed through artistic reproduction, is no sweet, utopian vision. Life in these places is not easy, and these photographs show us what an effort they must make to exist. We are not shown this explicitly. but it is not hard for us to imagine what it takes them to bring drinking water back to the maloca (communal hut), the grueling task of stunning a few little fish in muddy igarapés (bayous) to supplement their diet, the agility required to kill a restless paca (large nocturnal rodent - Coniculus paca) with a spear or collect enough of the right feathers to make a ceremonial headdress.

Rodrigo uses black and white photographs - symbolizing the few choices that fate offers these small cultures - to reveal that which is hidden and remote, elevating it to the category of real and existent. Looking at these images, sometimes cruel in their beautiful poetry of shadows, fragments of the mirror of time left behind among clearings and villages, we can't deny the life and the ties that connect Indians to their specific territory. It is no longer possible to speak only in conservationist terms of sustainability, of respectfully exploiting the jungle's natural resources, without taking into account the cultural impact on societies that have lived there for centuries. Thanks to the eye of Mapinguarí-Petrella, indigenous communities get unexpected visibility in this fateful drama, a real-life drama in which most of the inhabitants are not even aware of the danger surrounding them.

We don't know what the future will bring for them, and the outlook is not good. But knowing the disastrous effects, even on their health, of direct contact between their cultures and ours, between them and us, we must be more generous and careful, because nothing absolutely nothing justifies the damage that we cause. Surely, cultural contamination is inevitable; in fact, we can see in Petrella's photographs an Indian wearing a digital watch - perhaps a mere adornment - though the rest of his attire does not clash one bit with that of his community. I ask myself why he wants to know what time it is in a world ruled by the Sun and the Moon, in a world where this way of measuring the passage of time means nothing to the rest of his people.

Costumes with leaves, painted bodies, shaved heads, bodoques (ornaments) pierced through lower lips, modified teeth, beautiful feather adornments... The emperor of Tawantinsuyu, Túpac Inca Yupanqui, wanted to penetrate the Amazon Jungle to expand his empire. It was always thought that he abandoned this project in order to stifle an internal rebellion in the Collas province. Recently, however, pyramids and a city have been discovered in the Parima range, part of the Gurupira mountain system, near the source of the Padauiri, a tributary of the Rio Negro. They have yet to be excavated, but all indicators suggest they are Incan. Who knows the magnitude of the cultural contamination bean the Incas and these cultures?

Amazonian people have very different material values than Westerners. They place particular importance on the extraordinary feathers used to make ceremonial cocars (headdresses) and other ornaments indicating rank, ankle and wrist bracelets. Gold. silver and precious stones are worthless to them; they use the back-strap loom and Neolithic weapons as the Incas did and don't obsess over fossil fuels.

The Amazon Jungle and our entire planet depend on water, and this basin is the largest freshwater reserve in the world. Waters - gems more precious to us than all the gold and silver combined. Waters filtered by uncontaminated minerals that transmit the crystalline properties of diamonds, the pale blue of aquamarine, the emerald green of the unexplored jungle and the soft yellow of the beryl used to make the magical spectacles of the sad and beautiful fairy Melusine. Locked up in the tower of her castle in Lusignan, she watched, every Saturday, how the lower half of her body would turn into an aquatic animal. Isolated from everyone, no one could see her in this state, interrupting her bath, or she would automatically turn into a dragon and disappear forever, which is exactly what happened in the end.

The jungle and primeval forest contain countless secrets and treasures for science, health, and life that have yet to be discovered. But we can't enter just like that, all of a sudden. If We burst in without warning, without preparing her for our entry, we will turn her into a dragon; she will disappear, flying away like the sad Melusine, leaving behind nothing but sand.

The good savage and the friendly beast do not exist. Their tough existence, happy or sad, like for everyone else who inhabits the blue planet, has become extremely complicated. Kayapó, Kuikuro, Parintintin, Mamaindê, Marubo, Pirahã, Carauarí, Xavante, Sateré - Mawé, Mayoruna and many other peoples who live all over this vast territory, must assume the role of guardians of this lush grove; the role of the Angel Uriel who protects the gates to Eden, defending with his fiery sword what remains of so-called paradise so that all won't be lost, so that their beautiful daughters won't win the love of the pink boto (river dolphin), which turns into a handsome youth at sunset, but disappears as soon as the sun comes up.

We stopped dreaming and believing in magic and fairies a long time ago. Middle-class evasions/fantasies are now fulfilled in the Mayan Riviera or on *cruises with deluxe buffets and air conditioning down the Nile or the Amazon, for example. No one will see through the fairy Melusine's beryl glasses ever again, because they were made by a spell of faith in a world ruled by Newton's laws; they belong to a past order that will never be reinstated. That's why we will never be able to recognize the song of the Wirapurú bird that would give us dreamt-of desire in love, nor will we ever believe that the lovely "eyes" of the Guaraná fruit are those of a bewitched child.*

Some sources say that the Mapinguarí was a shaman who turned into a monster when the secret of his immortality was discovered. It does not matter: the myth is still alive, and therefore under constant construction. It takes us back to a time frame that doesn't coincide with ours; something that does not, however, make it inferior. It is merely different: it is theirs. Whether or not the creature is proven to exist is of little importance; the important thing is that the inhabitants of the Amazon are afraid of it an are very wary about wandering alone through the jungle, particularly on holy days, which is when they say it likes to attack. I wish I could protect them a little longer, at least until a way out is found for them. Let's hope that Rodrigo Petrella's excellent photographs will continue to capture our attention, showing us the beauty of these bodies and faces, in themselves and by themselves, as he fends off unwanted invaders with his Mapinguarí camera.

Amador Griñó Andres

COIAB

Coordination of Indigenous Organizations of the Brazilian Amazon (COIAB)

COIAB, Coordination of Indigenous Organizations of the Brazilian Amazon, is the country's largest indigenous coalition. It is comprised of 200 member organizations from all nine states of the Brazilian Amazon local associations, regional federations, organizations of indigenous women, of indigenous teachers and students. COIAB brings together approximately 60% of the country's indigenous population. Seeking to preserve and promote the sustainability of the peoples and their territories, COIAB acts in three fundamental arenas: the indigenous peoples rights to the traditional territories, public policies that relate to indigenous issues and land management by professional indigenous people.

The Amazonian Indigenous Peoples

Millions of Brazilians of different origins live in diverse ecosystems in the sprawling Brazilian Amazon. A majority face challenges in the areas of health, education, work, housing, and diet. Add to these challenges the cultural diversity of Brazil; there are - among others, the indigenous peoples, the black population, the caboclos - and you can understand why it is the embracing of plurality and challenge that characterizes the sense of belonging in this country. Plurality abounds within the indigenous population as well. There are more than 160 Almazonian indigenous peoples, totaling an estimated population of 440 thousand. They live on 422 indigenous lands, which correspond to 22% of the Amazonian territory - nearly 267 million acres.

Various indigenous peoples have been contacted by people from western cultures, beginning in the 1500's with the first period of colonization of Brazil, to the present day. These interactions have had a huge impact on the indigenous peoples' original life-styles. Many of those surviving exposure to western influences, left behind their tradition of foraging to settle into villages. There, their foraging skills were useless and they found they were immediately faced with the reduction of essential resources for their survival. Today, despite the contact with non-indigenous technologies, globalization and extraordinary economic growth, the Amazonian peoples still live off hunting, fishing and other kinds of extracting from the forest, and small farms, still mainly working 'and living in small family groups. The small number of people and the high proportion of children limit how much land they can cultivate and how much they can extract from the forest. In the case of the small farms (roças), the surplus is sometimes sold or traded in nearby towns, giving people some means to purchase other basic commodities.

Among the Amazonian indigenous peoples, an estimated 69 autonomous peoples prefer to live in isolation and don't have any contact with the surrounding communities. Understanding the need to preserve the autonomy of this isolated Amazonian population, COIAB is especially involved in protecting these peoples' rights, particularly their land-use rights.

Today, the great challenges faced by the indigenous peoples of Amazonia derive from their relationship with the land and nature: in the face of the western definition of progress, they strive to maintain a respect for a life-style developed throughout thousands of years of forest life, to keep separate and to preserve their territories, to protect their food sources and to search for sustainable economic activities. The indigenous peoples' survival strategy has always been to conserve biodiversity. They have always understood that excessive harvest of one element of the forest would destroy the delicate balance of all life in the forest. Thus, their ancient knowledge offers the rest of the world a model for a sustainable world.

COIAB and the Protection of Biodiversity

COIAB, along with other indigenous organizations, has been discussing alternative strategies that will protect the existing biodiversity in indigenous lands. The indigenous movement is aware of the important role this great natural heritage plays' in preserving our planet. A forest of this size affects climate change through its ability to absorb carbon, it holds a huge store of underground fresh water, and within its domain countless animal and plant species flourish that are found nowhere else on the planet. The forest must be preserved because it sustains all principles of life.

Guardians of the Forest

The exhibit "Guardians of the Forest" is COIAB's first initiative to present to the world the cultural wealth of the indigenous peoples and the peoples' efforts to preserve the ecosystem in which they live. The exhibit presents the expressions and life-styles of peoples such as the Mamaindê, Kuikuro, Kayapó, Tenharin, Ashaninka, Kashinawá, Shanenawa, Pareci, Xavante, Rikbaktsa, Enawenê-Nawê, Krahõ, Parintintin and Pirahã.

In spite of their skills and knowledge which allow them to survive and live in harmony in the forest, the indigenous peoples are still seriously threatened by the advancement of agribusiness, large infrastructure constructions and energy production in Amazonia. However, thanks to the peoples' resistance and capacity to protect their territories, the indigenous lands rest as green islands amidst the devastation, that has resulted from development strategies uncommitted to global equilibrium.

Rodrigo Petrella's beautiful photographs provide a doorway to the fantastic universe of the indigenous cultures. They are also a unique contribution to the efforts to preserve life in Amazon, beginning with the peoples who, as guardians of ancient knowledge and practices, are vital for the survival of all life on our planet.

Jecinaldo Sateré-Mawé

Coordinator - COIAB

The Guardians

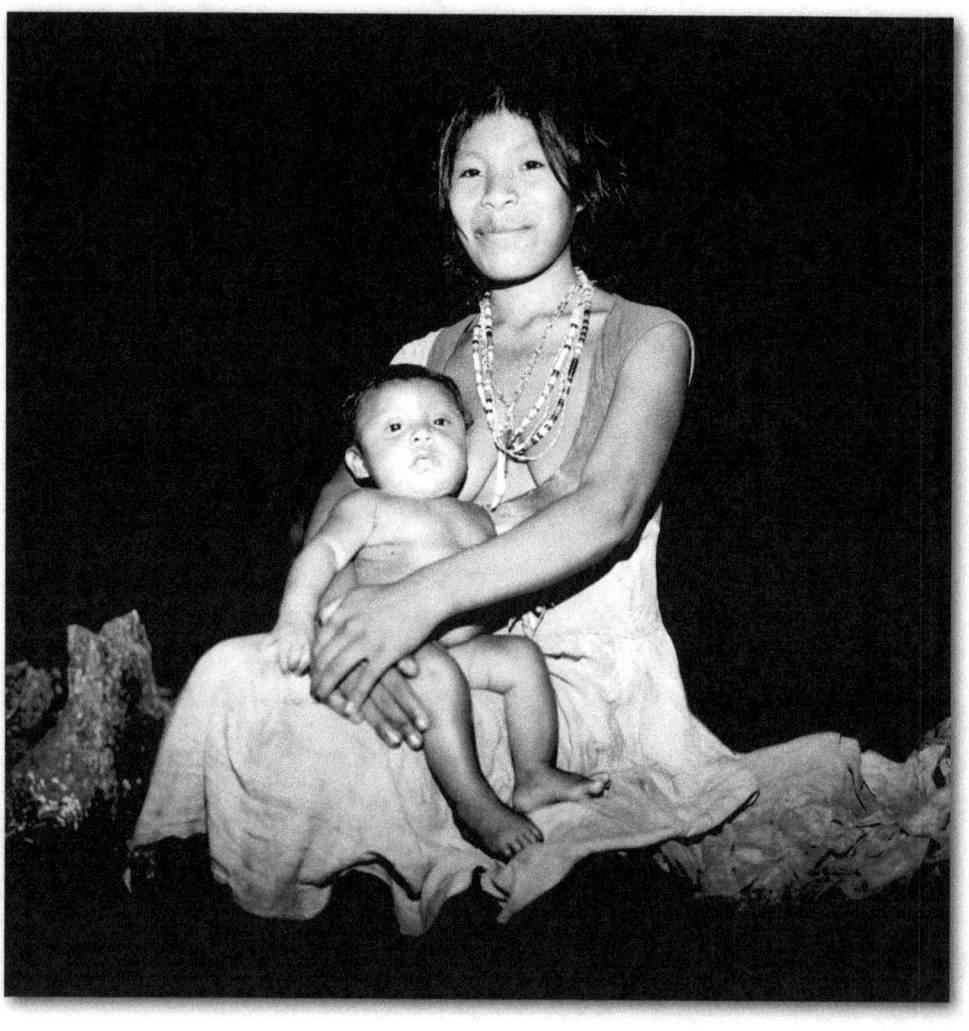

Pirahã / mother and child at the Uruapiara river

Pareci

The Pareci are a group of 2000 people living in many villages throughout the state of Mato Grosso. Their language belongs to the Aruak family, spoken from Paraguay, Bolivia and Peru to countries on the northern coast, such as Suriname, Guyana and Venezuela, drawing a big arc across the South American map.

The Pareci, self-styled halíti, meaning "people", have an old history of contact with the surrounding non-indigenous people. First reports date back to the late 17th century. In 1908, Colonel Rondon, who would later establish the Service of Indian Protection (Serviço de Proteção ao Índio, SPI), first met the Pareci while supervising the construction of a telegraph-line in the area. The contact was pacific, in contrast with what happened with the Nambikwara, who attacked Rondon's retinue.

It was in that same region that between the 1930s and the 1970s, an educational experiment took place, at a Jesuit mission called Utiariti (meaning "place of wise people"). The mission was focused on children, who were kept in an internship system, separated from their families and forbidden to speak their native languages, living under strict discipline. This system also affected, although each to a different extent, the Nambikwara, Irantxe, Pareci, Rikbáktsa, Apiaká and Kayabi people, leaving a permanent mark upon their identities.

In May 2004 I also had a pacific meeting with the Pareci, and I was able to photograph them in the villages of Formoso and Sacre. Living under the pressure of farming and economical advances which jeopardize their hunting and fishing activities, the Pareci now seek new sources of income. In a partnership with the non-indigenous populations who live nearby, the Pareci have started cultivating soybeans on indigenous lands —an activity that shall bring not only positive impacts (such as increased income), but also negative

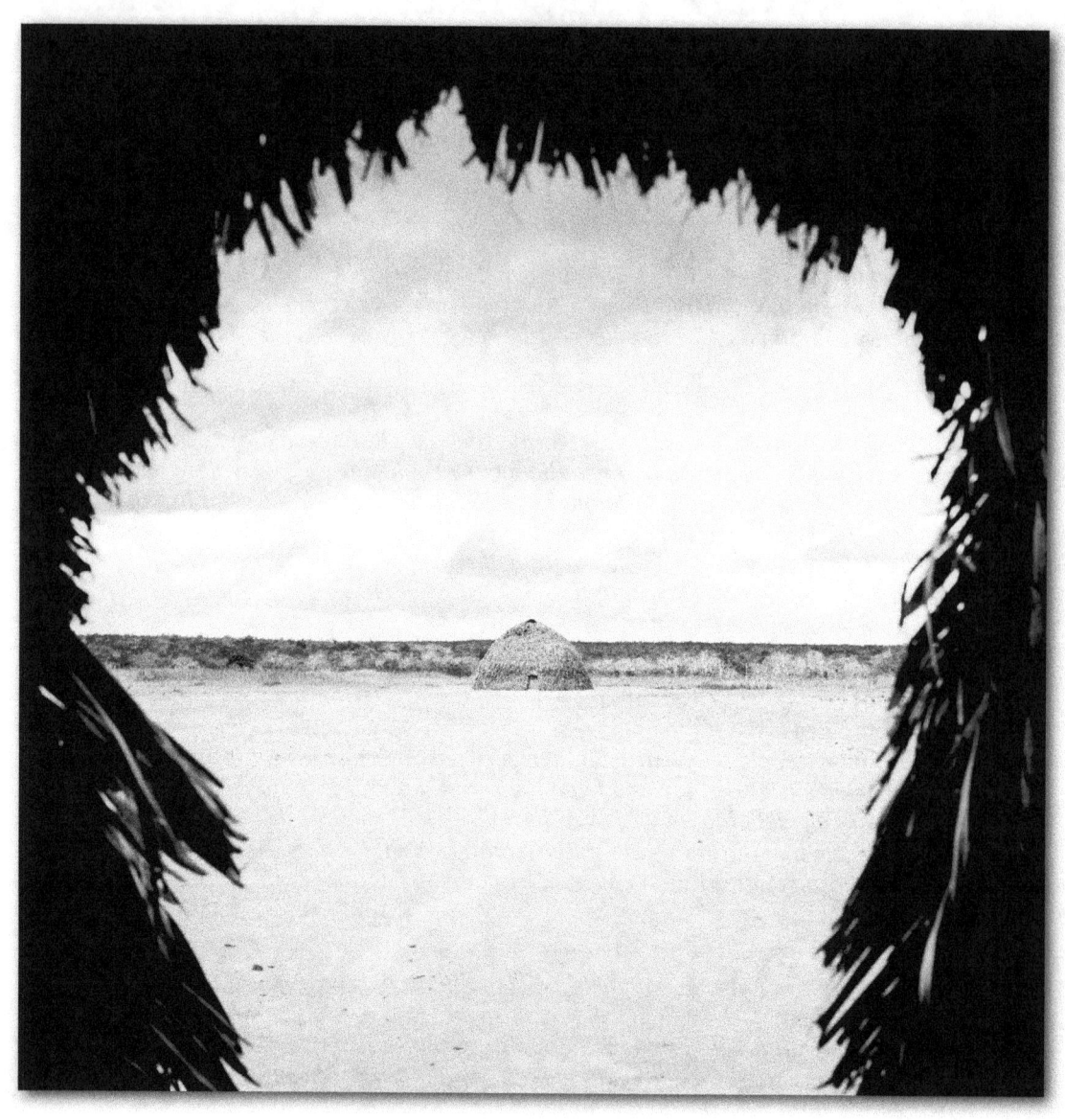

Parecí Maloca / Looking outside through the entrance

Pareci's Mesa - Mato Grosso 2004

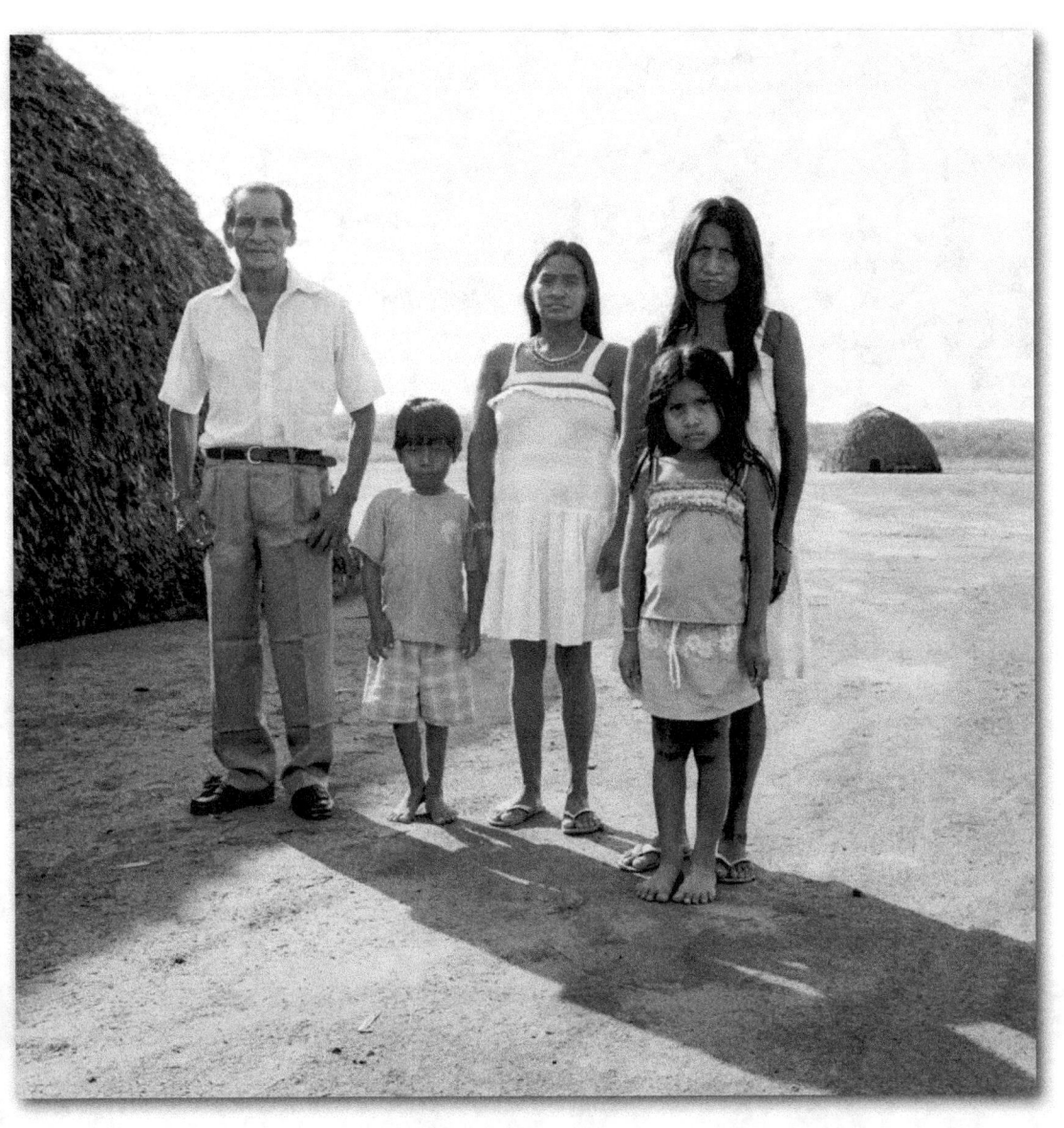

Family / Formal portrait at Sacrê community

2004

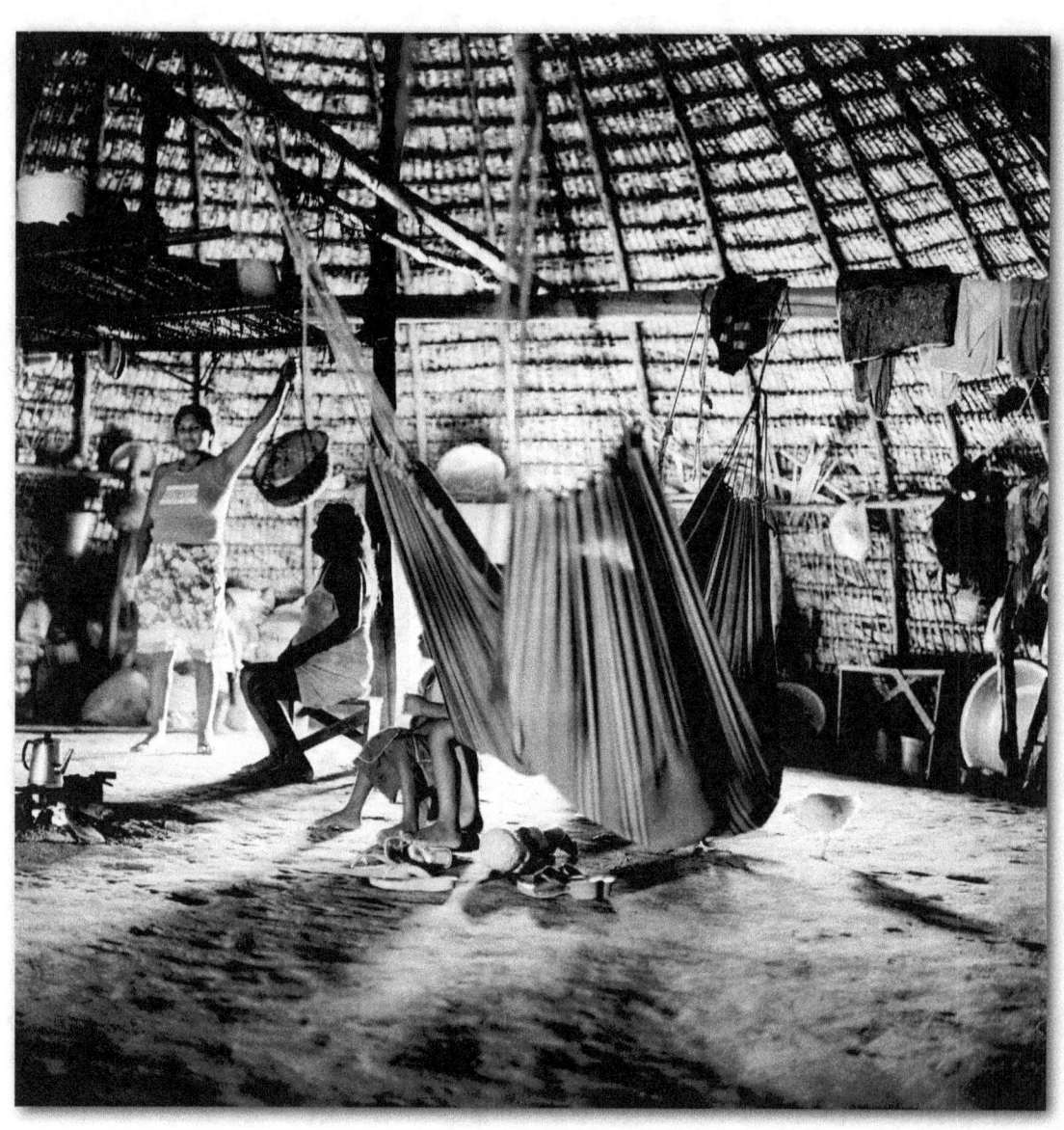

Formoso community / Afternoon kitchen talk

2004

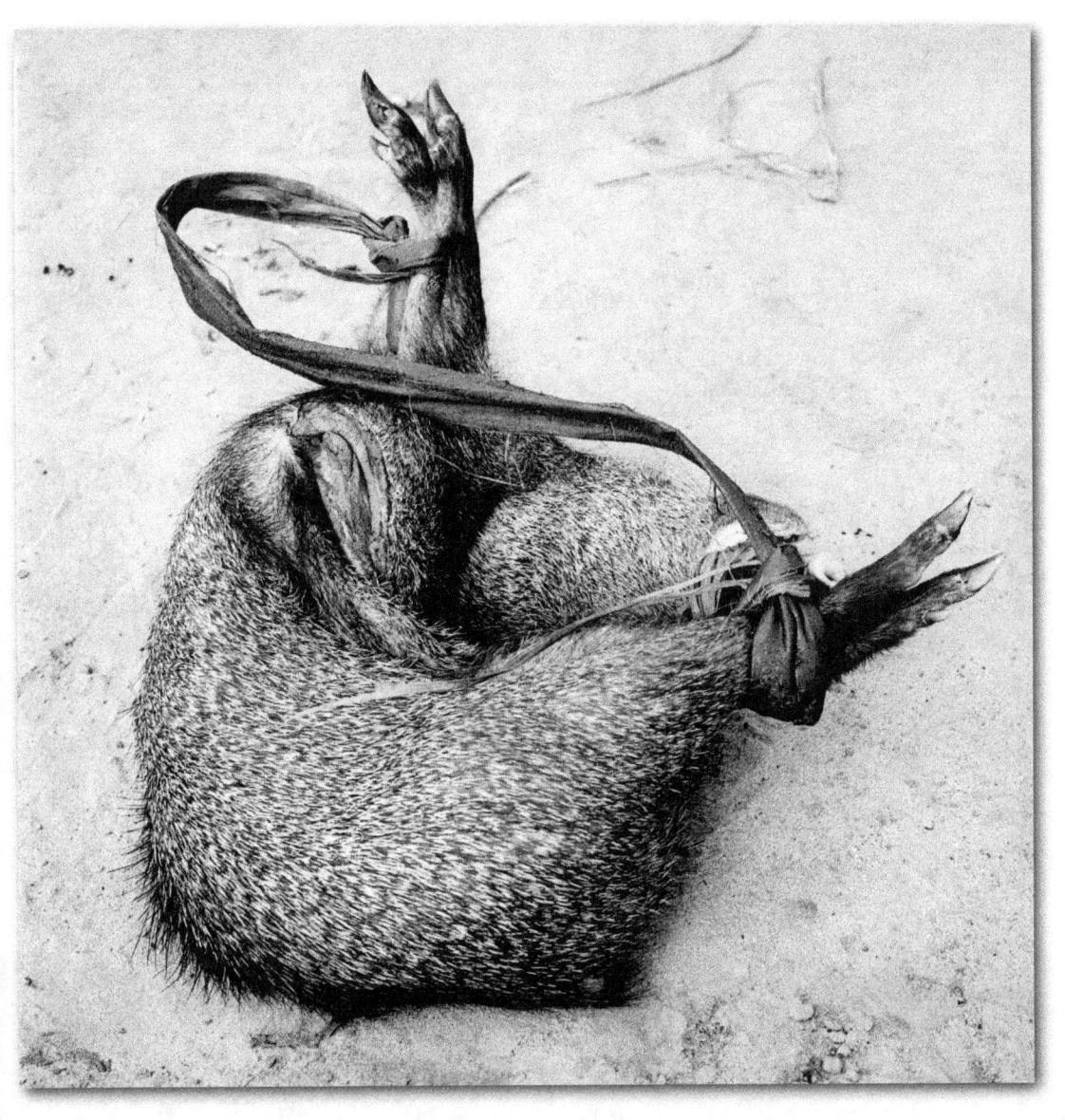

Eviscerated Queixada (Tayassu pecari)

2004

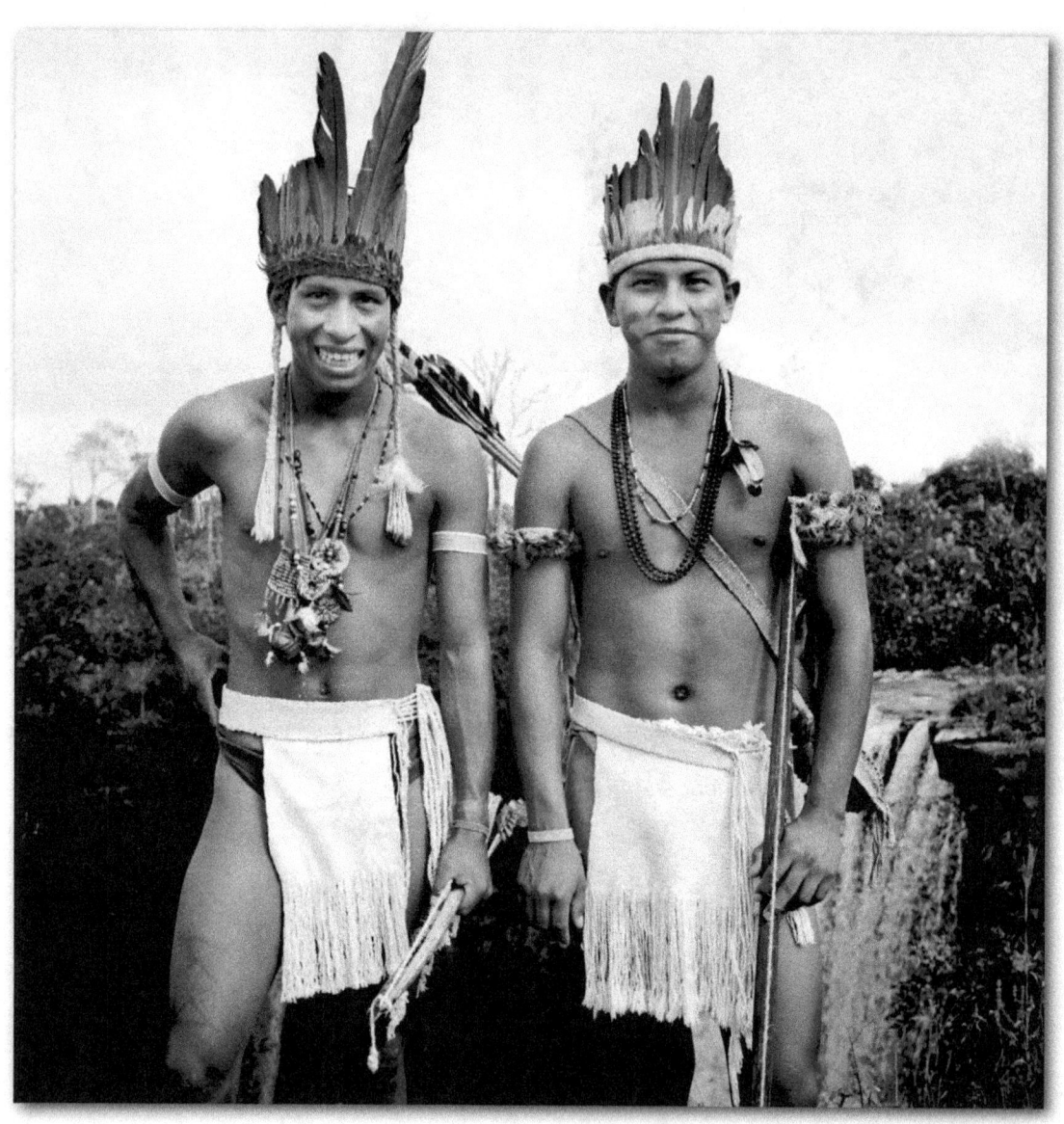

Warriors at the Formoso waterfalls / Tradicional style

2004

Alto-Xingú

The Xingu Indigenous Park (XIP) was the first big portion of land to be demarcated as an indigenous territory in Brazil, devised by the Villas-Bôas brothers and officialized by President Jânio Quadros in 1961. The Xingu Park and three adjacent indigenous lands —Pequizal do Naruvôtu, Wawi and Batovi, which were demarcated later— together form the Indigenous Land of Xingu, a territory where approximately 8000 people from 16 different ethnicities live.

High Xingu is a multi-ethnic and multilingual sociocultural complex in the southern area of the park. It is inhabited by 10 different indigenous peoples who speak languages ranging from three distinct linguistic branches, to an isolated language —the Mehináku, Wauja and Yawalapití (speakers of Aruak languages); Kalapalo, Nahukuá, Kuikuro and Matipú (speakers of Karib languages); Kamayurá and Aweti (speakers of Tupi languages); and the Trumai (speakers of an isolated language). Despite their linguistic diversity, these ethnicities share characteristics such as the circular shape of their villages, certain aspects of their material cultures, body painting and some myths and rituals, such as the famous Kuarup.

The Kuarup is a funerary ritual performed by peoples from High Xingu in honor of deceased chiefs, who are paid homage in the form of wooden effigies. Distinct peoples perform this funerary celebration, in which the spirit of a notable person leaves the village represented by a tree trunk, heading towards the underworld, thus putting an end to the family's mourning period. The etymology of the name of the ritual, 'Kuarup', originates from the Kuarup tree.

In August 2005 I had the opportunity to attend the Kuarup in the Ipatse village, from the Kuikuro ethnicity. It was the farewell ritual of two important leaders whose names must not be spoken, deceased two months before. I also took pictures in the same village in September 2007.

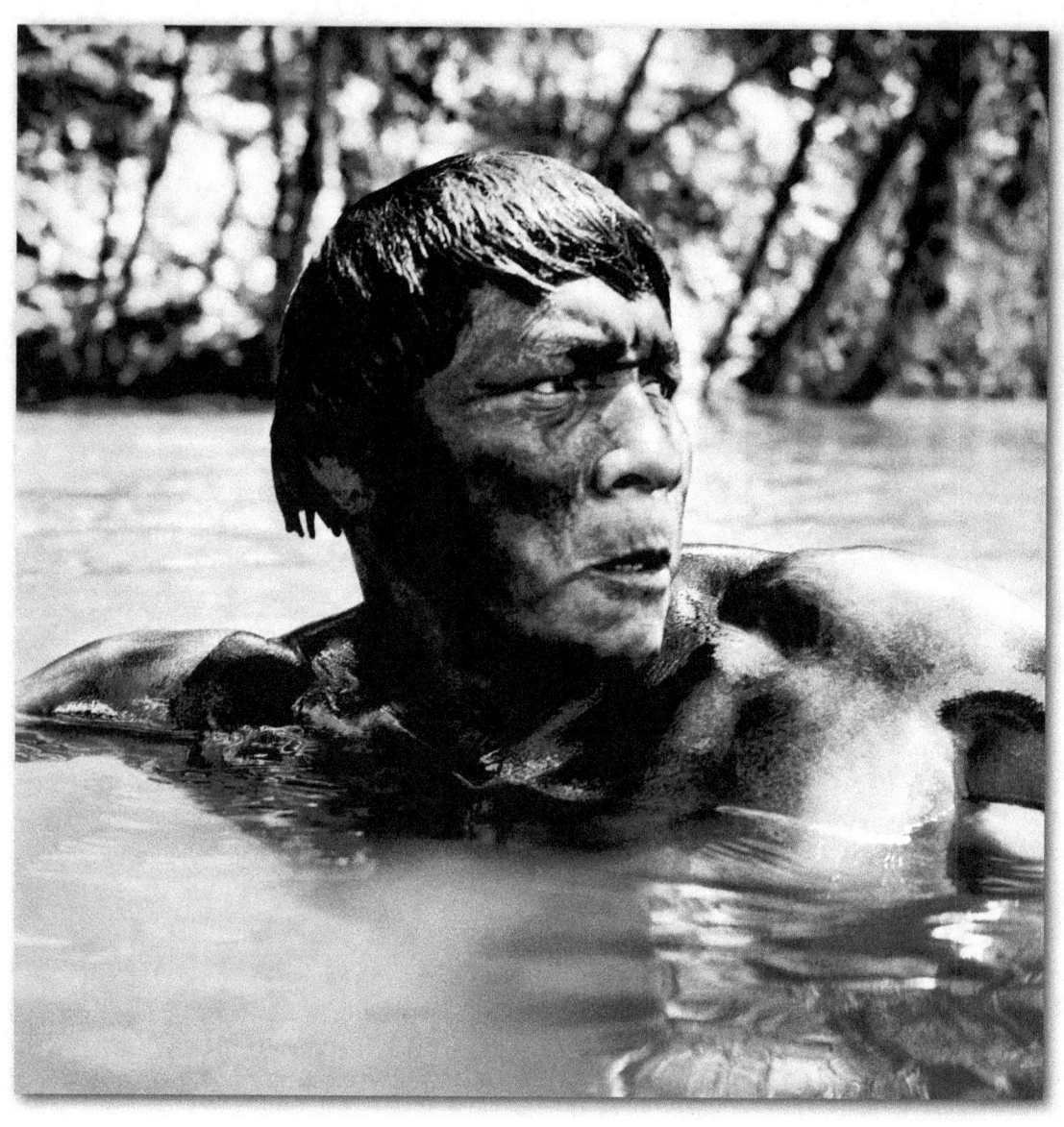

Kuikuro warrior / Fishing for the Kuarup celebration

Alto Xingú / Mato Grosso 2005

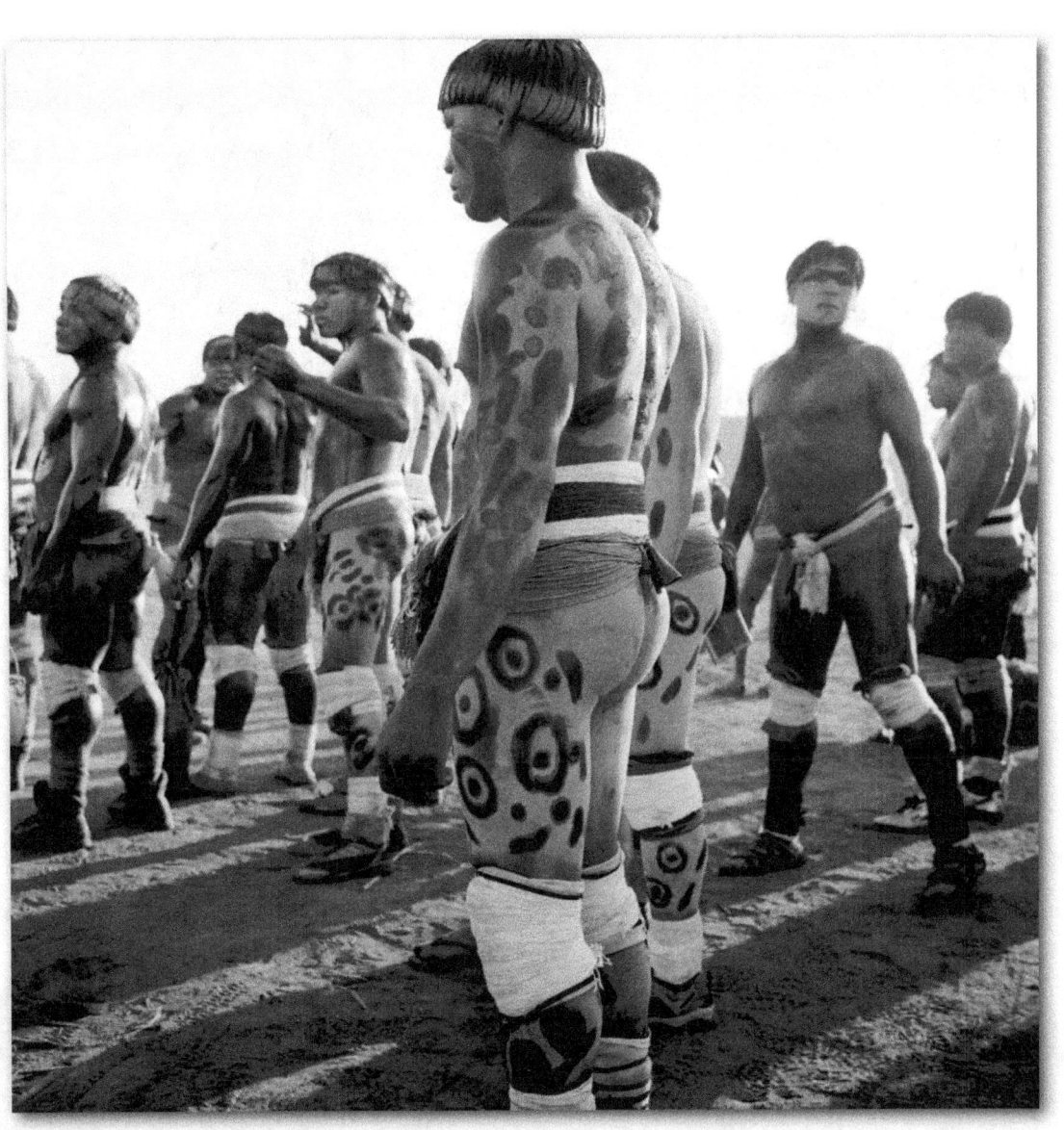

Fighters in preparation for the Huka-Huka (Grappling fight)

2005

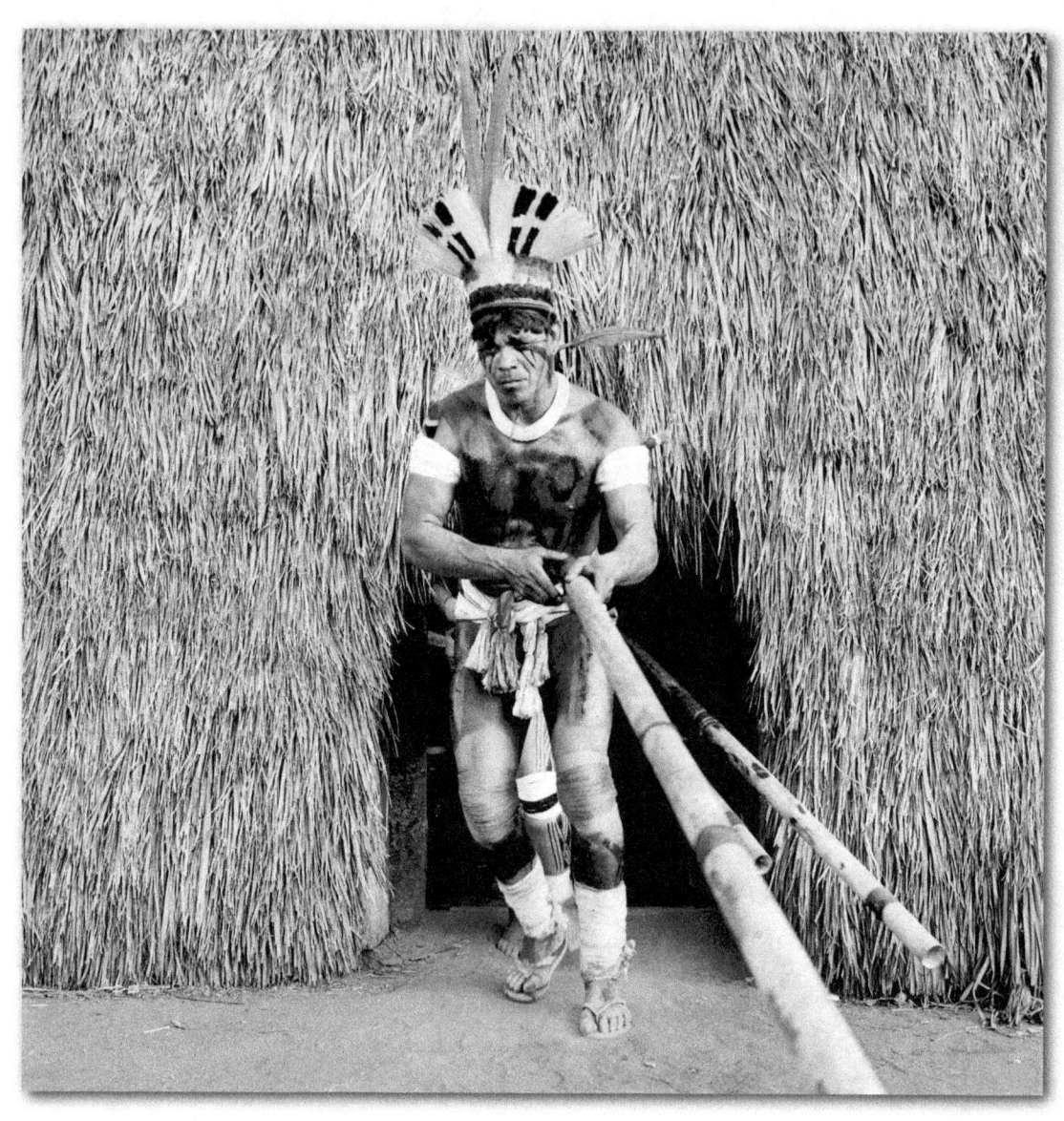

Uruá Flute / Made of a pair of single tone bamboos (aprox. 6 feet)

2005

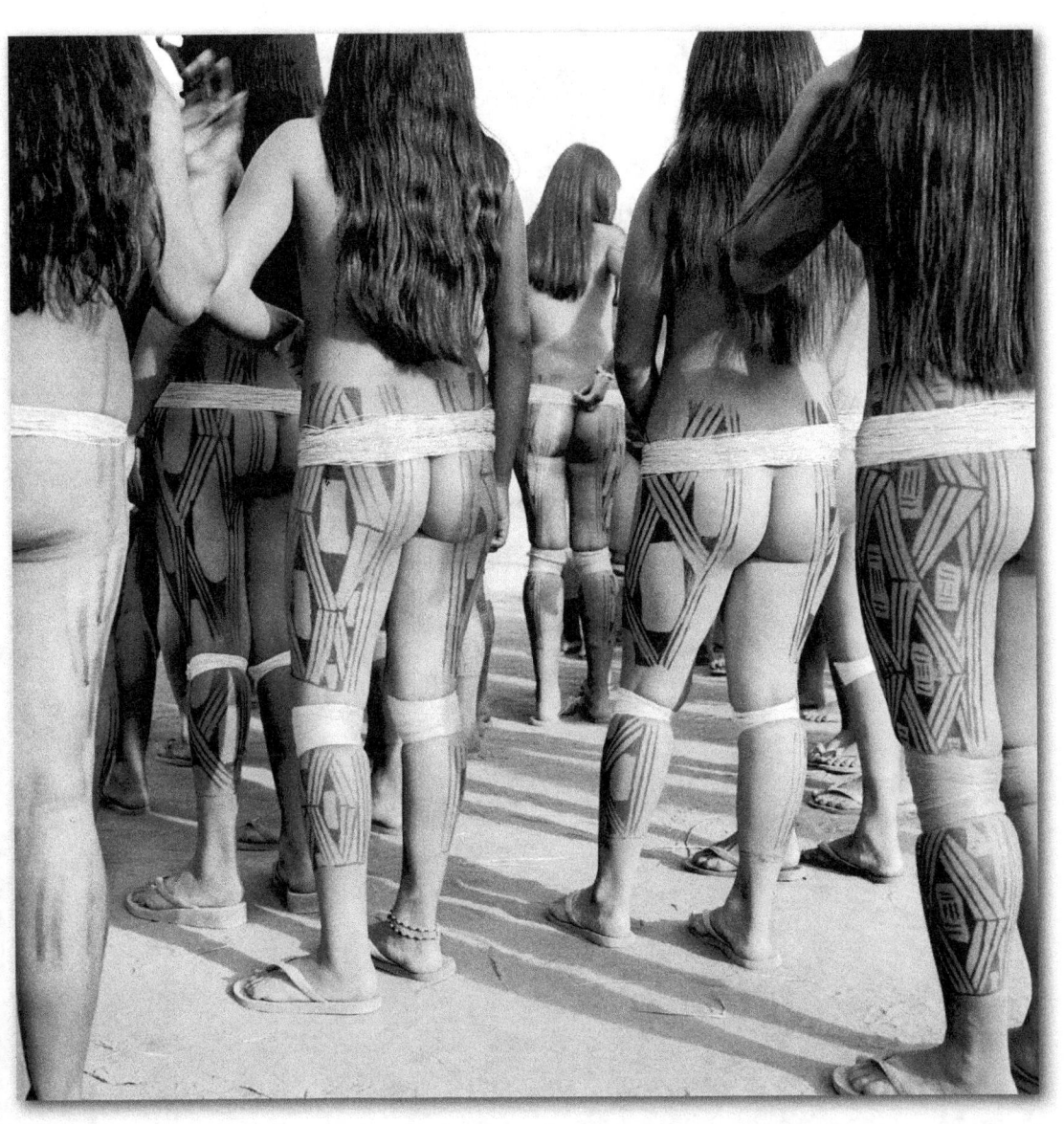

Girls small talk, wachting the Huka -Huka fighters

2005

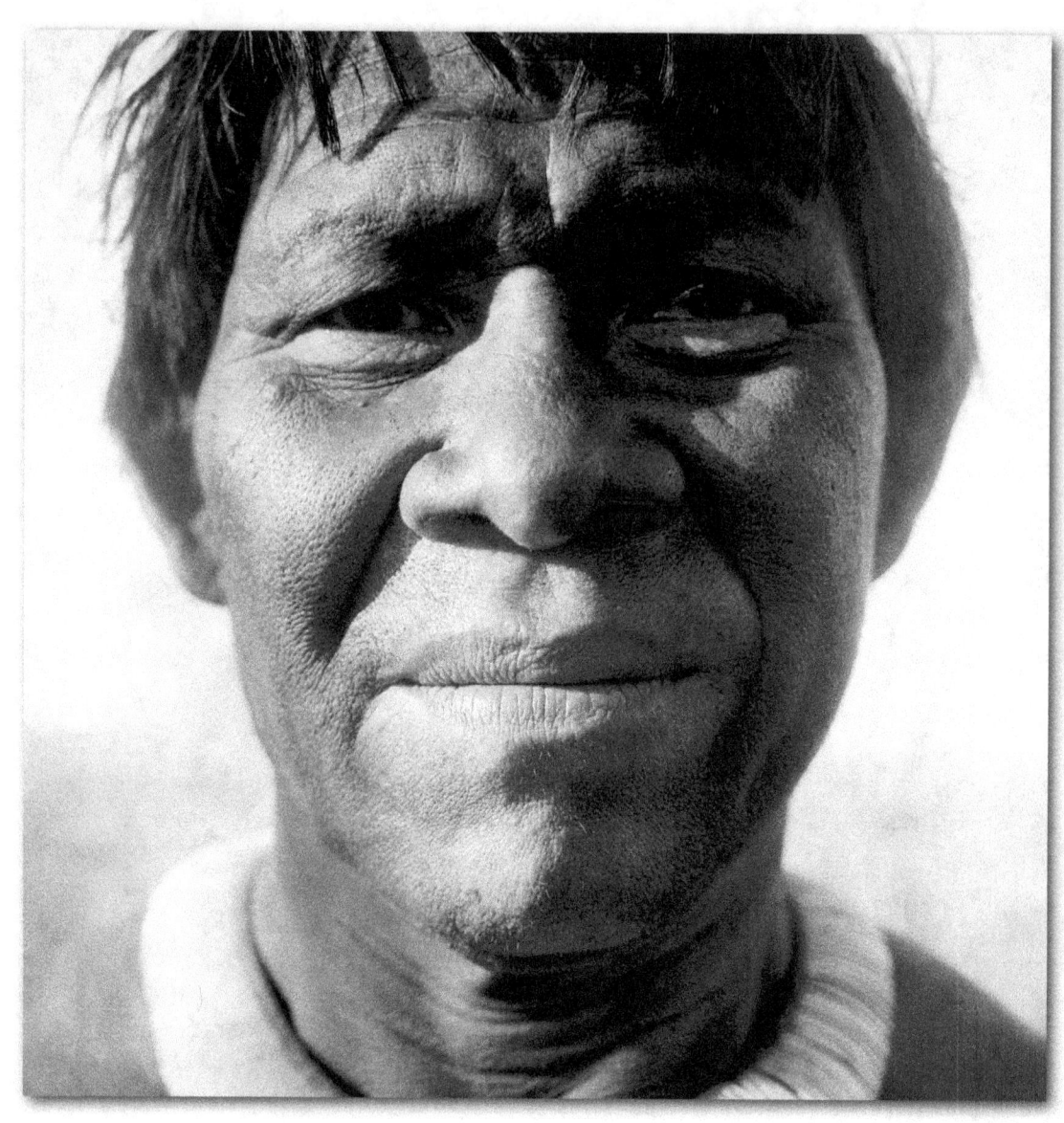

Tagó / Kuikuro shaman

2005

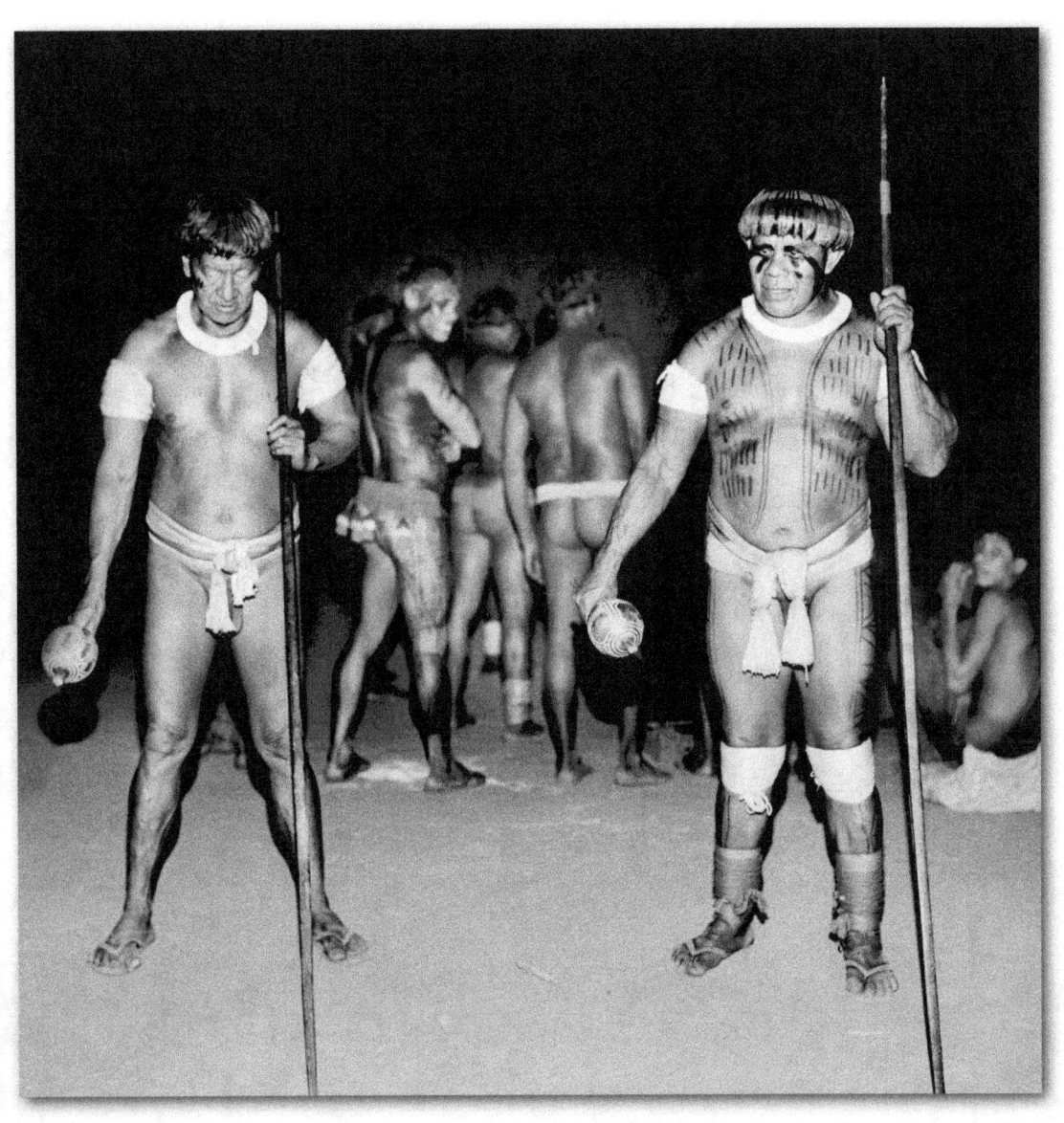

Shamans chanting for the spirts / Night before the final event

2005

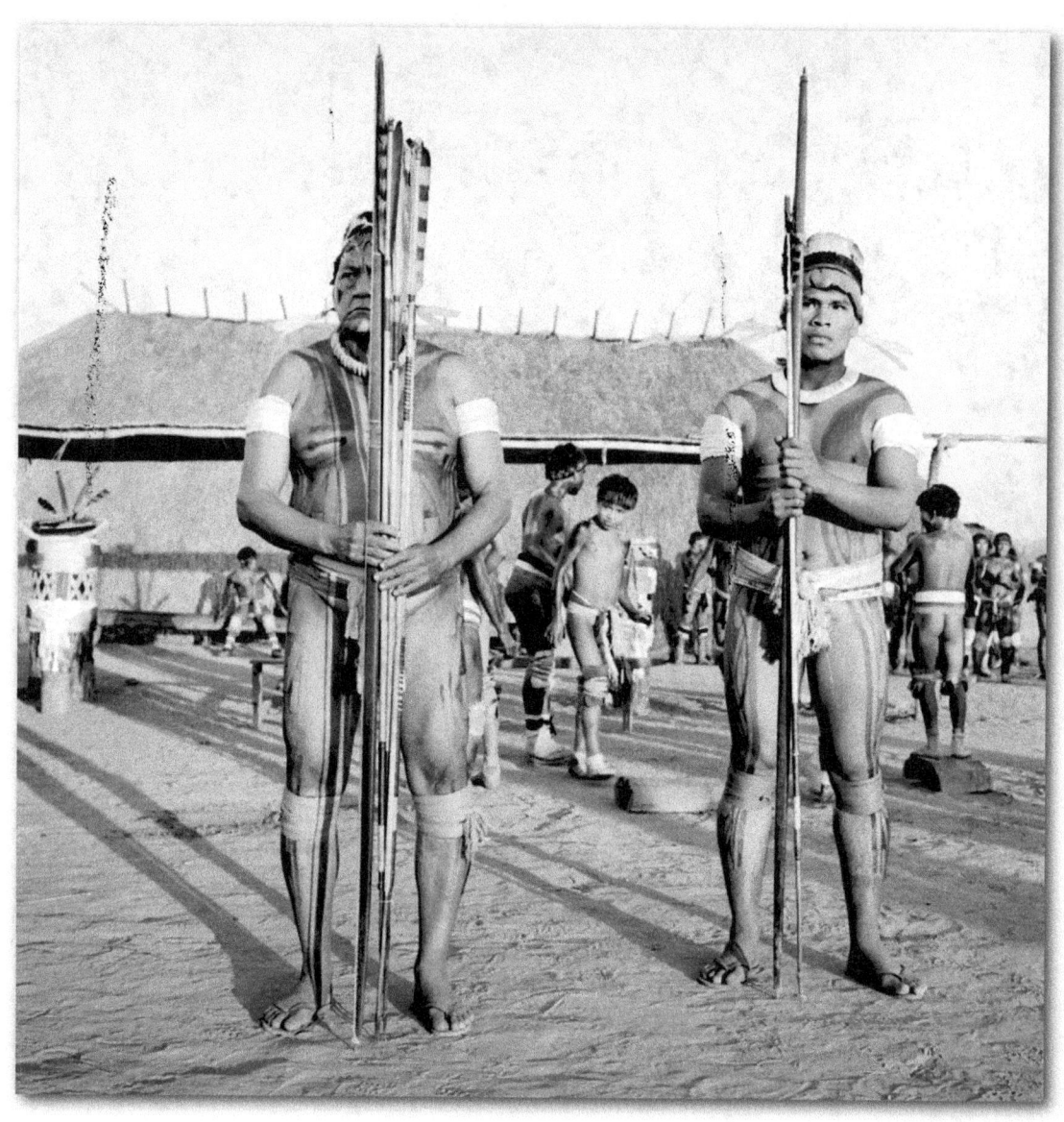

Jakalo attending his father Kuarup (left size)

2005

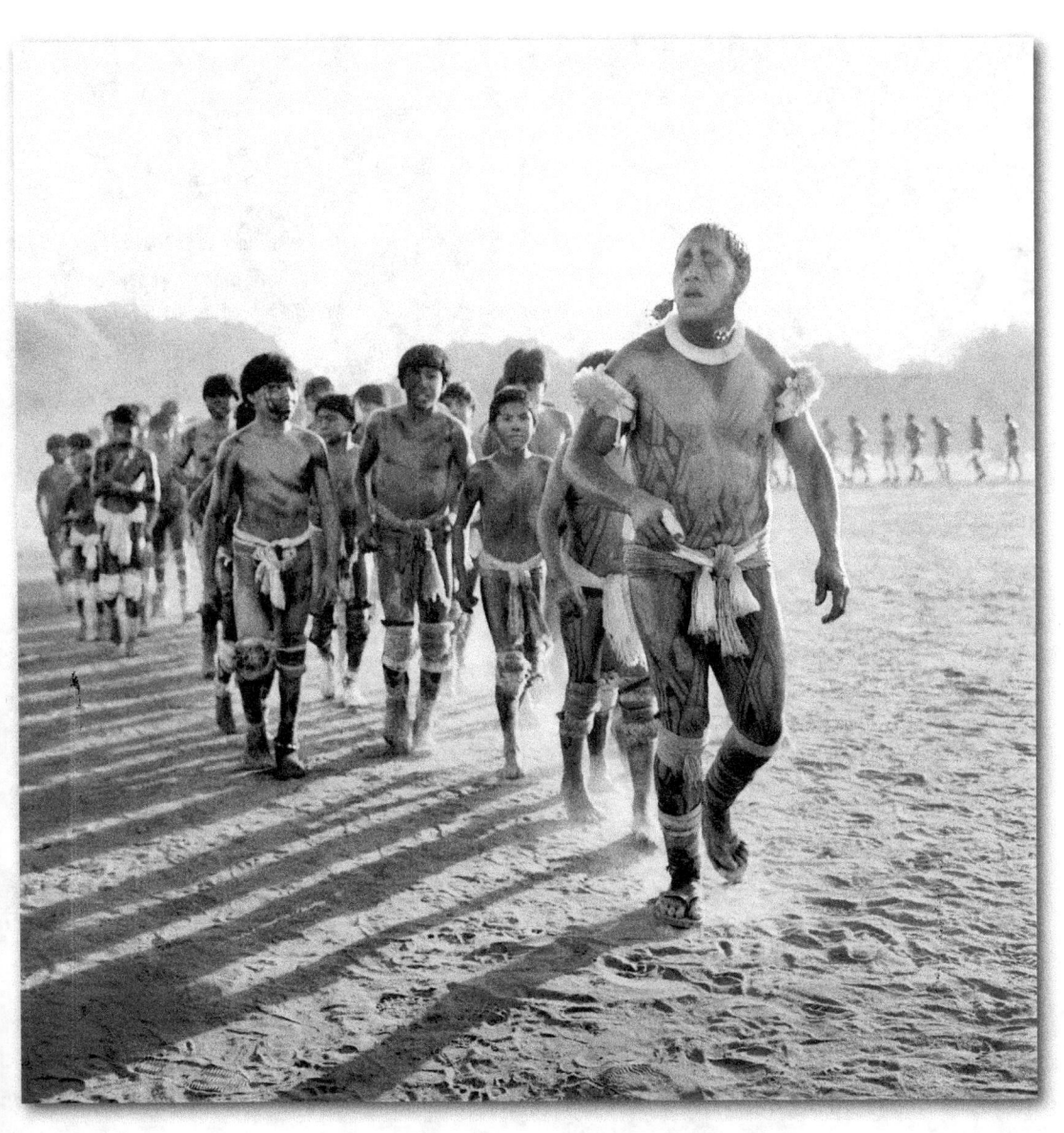

Ipatse community

2005

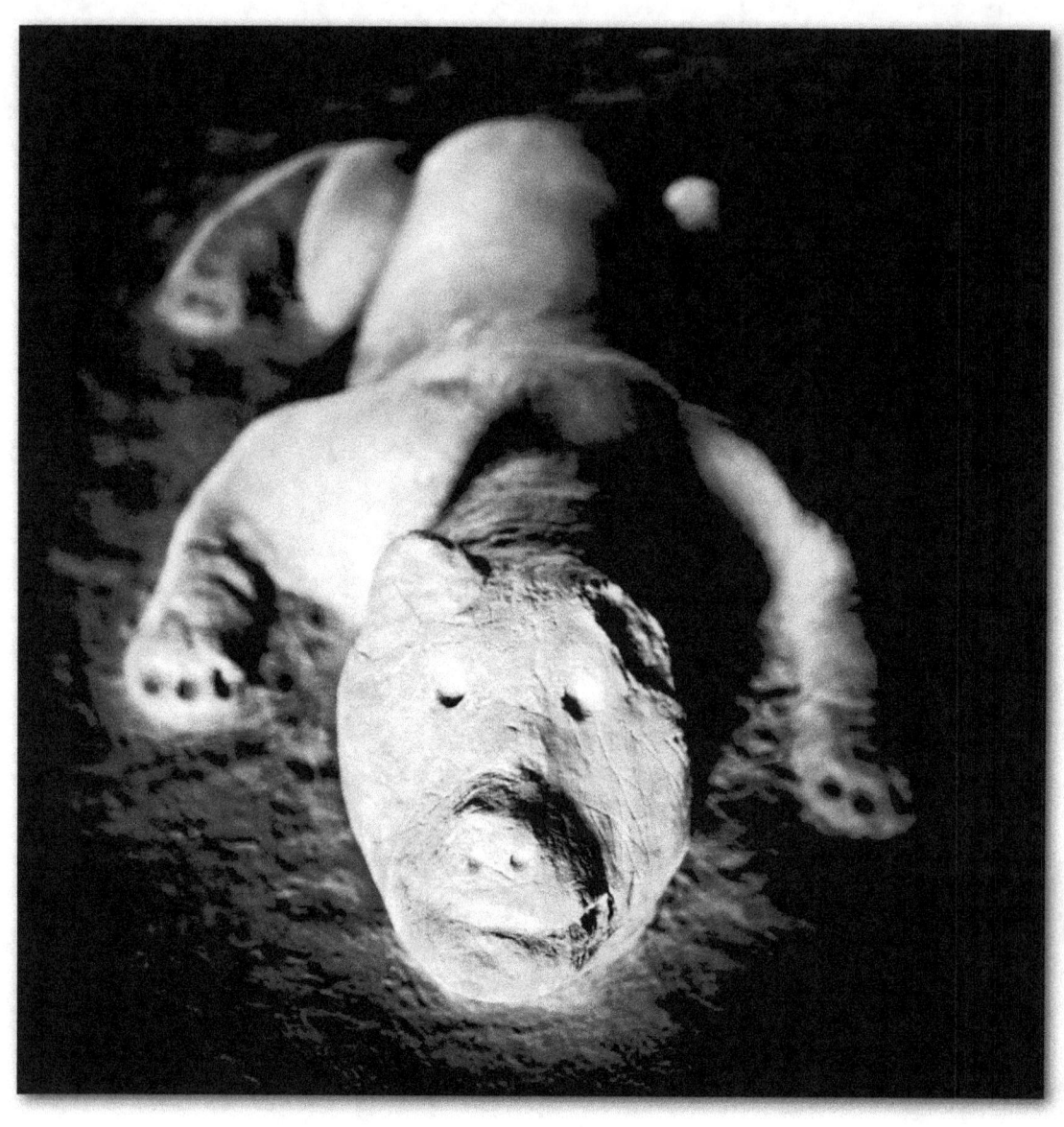

Jaguar / Clay sculpture inside chief Afukaká's house

2005

Nambikwara

The Nambikwara people encompasses indigenous groups living in three different areas which together form its territory: Serra do Norte, Chapada dos Parecis and Vale do Guaporé. The name, which comes from the Tupi-Guarani branch, is a generic term that designates approximately 17 subgroups*. Living in the northwestern region of Mato Grosso state as well as parts of Rondônia state, the Nambikwara are all speakers of Nambikwara languages. Their languages are divided into three linguistic groups —Sabanê, Northern Nambikwara and Southern Nambikwara— and belong to a linguistic branch unrelated to any other South American language. The Nambikwara Mamaindê, a subgroup living in the northern area of their territory, were the first ethnicity I had the opportunity to visit. I came back to their villages many other times, especially to Capitão Pedro village, named after a chief murdered in 1993.

The nose piercing ritual —which serves as a permanent marker of the passing from adolescence to adulthood— was then falling into oblivion. It hadn't been performed by that group since 1984, and few were the ones who knew how to do it. I reminded them many times of the importance of keeping their traditions alive and, after a 24-year hiatus, on a cold winter morning in 2008, they decided to resume the practice. The low temperatures increased the pain involved in the piercing process, which was conducted using something like a very sharp wooden dagger, all of which contributed to make the scene all the more intense. We celebrated a few days later, when we spent half a day walking to a distant cave in order to hunt bats, a local delicacy. Carved out in a mountain between a plateau and the Guaporé Valley sierra and covered with native vegetation, the cave represents the portal that is the site of the passage of souls between worlds, where spirits go when people die —spirits that may return in the body of humans or animals.

*To the north live the Sabanê, Txawenté, Txawanté, Yalakunté, Yalakaloré, Latundê, Hinkatesu (Manduca), Mamaindê e Negarotê; at the plateau Wakalitesu, Halotesu, Kithaulhu e Sawentesu; at the valley Aikkutesu, Nantesu, Qalisattesu, Yxotxusu, Elahitxansu, Alantesu, Alakatesu, Waikatesu, Wasusu e Katitaulhu. The latter being composed of four local groups: Galitsu, Haluhwaisu, Waihlatisu e Sayulikisu.

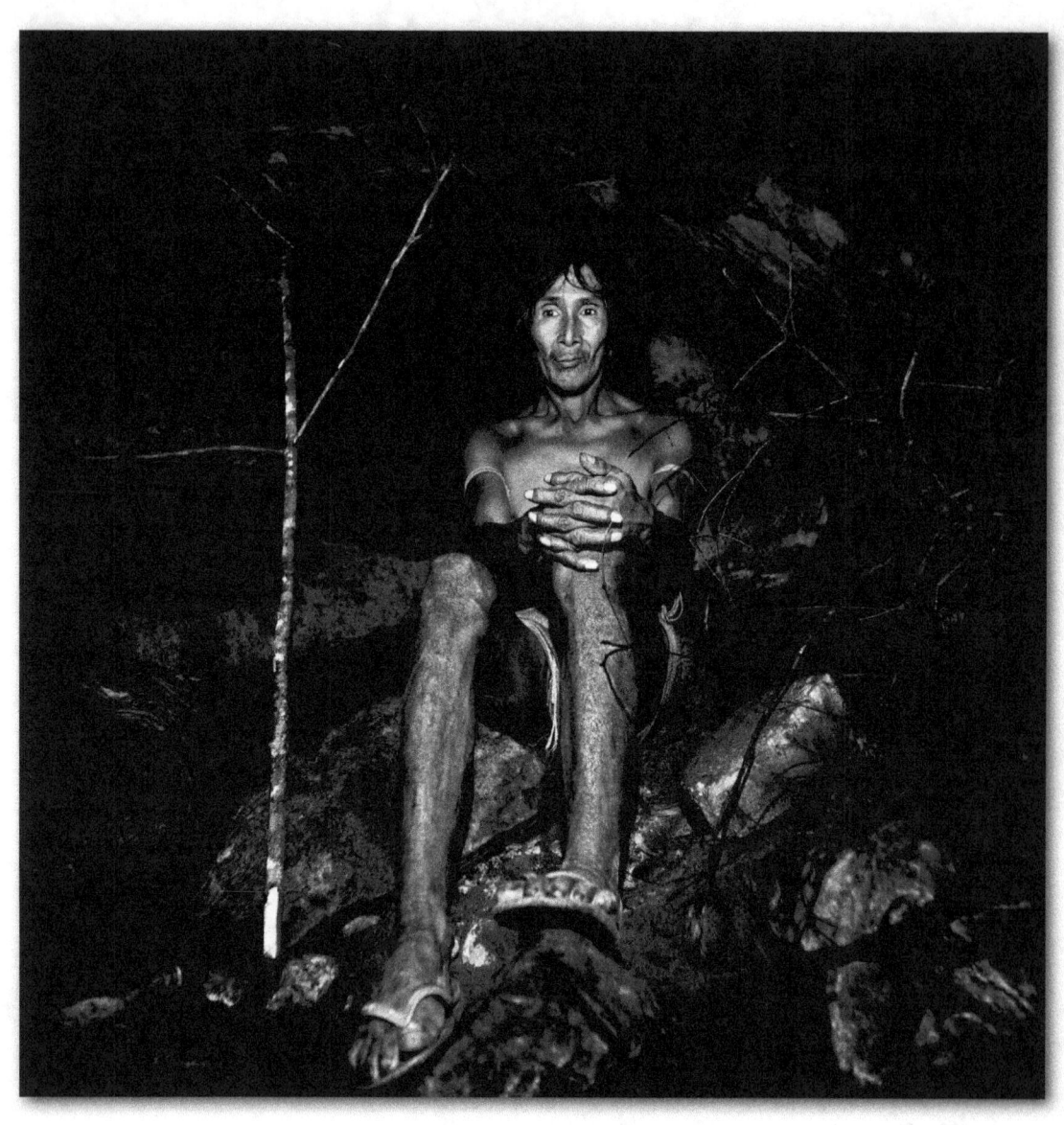

Jacy Shaman / Trance inside the sacred cave

Guaporé Valley / Rondônia 2008

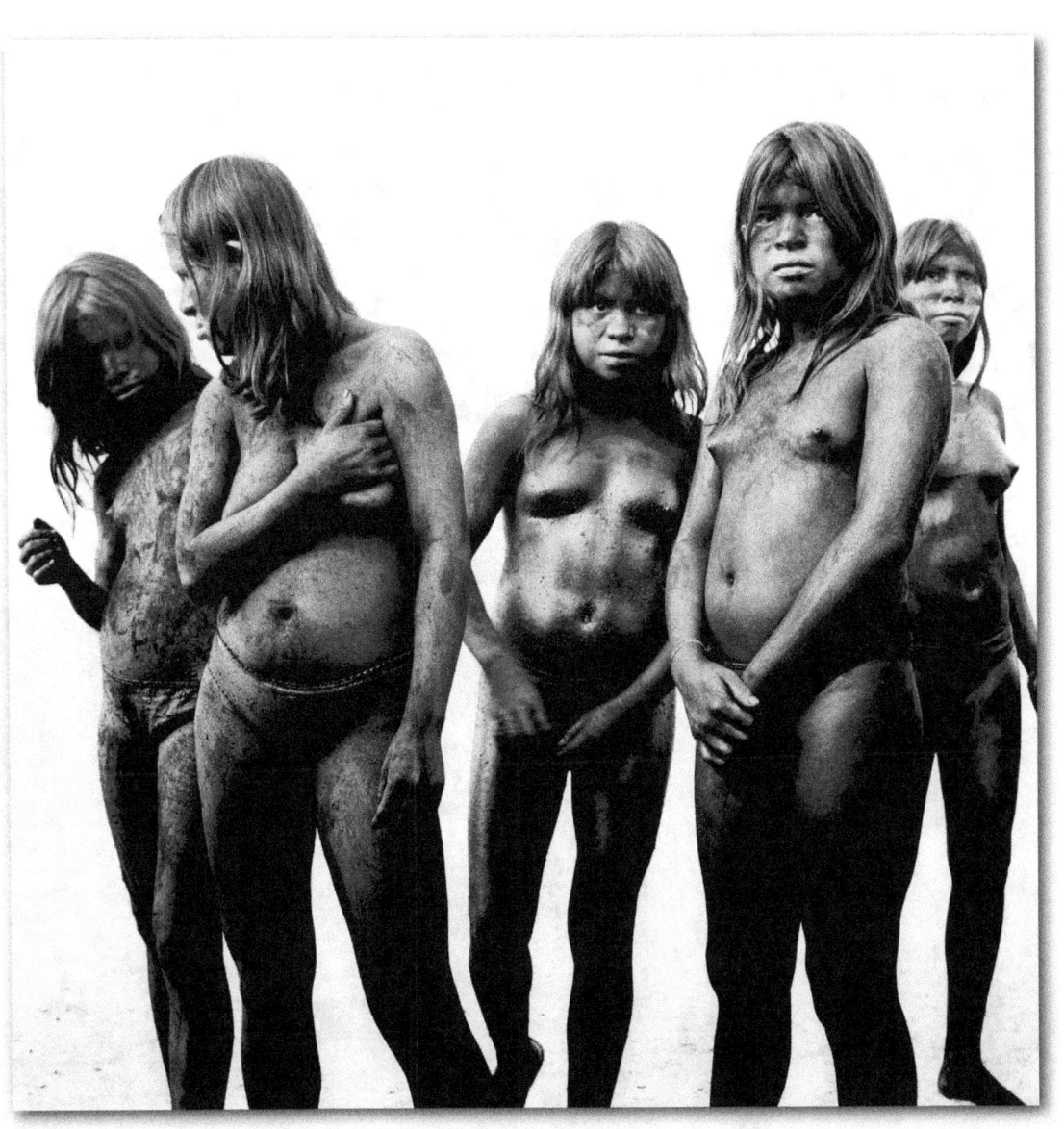

Mamainde Girls / Smeared in coal ashes

2008

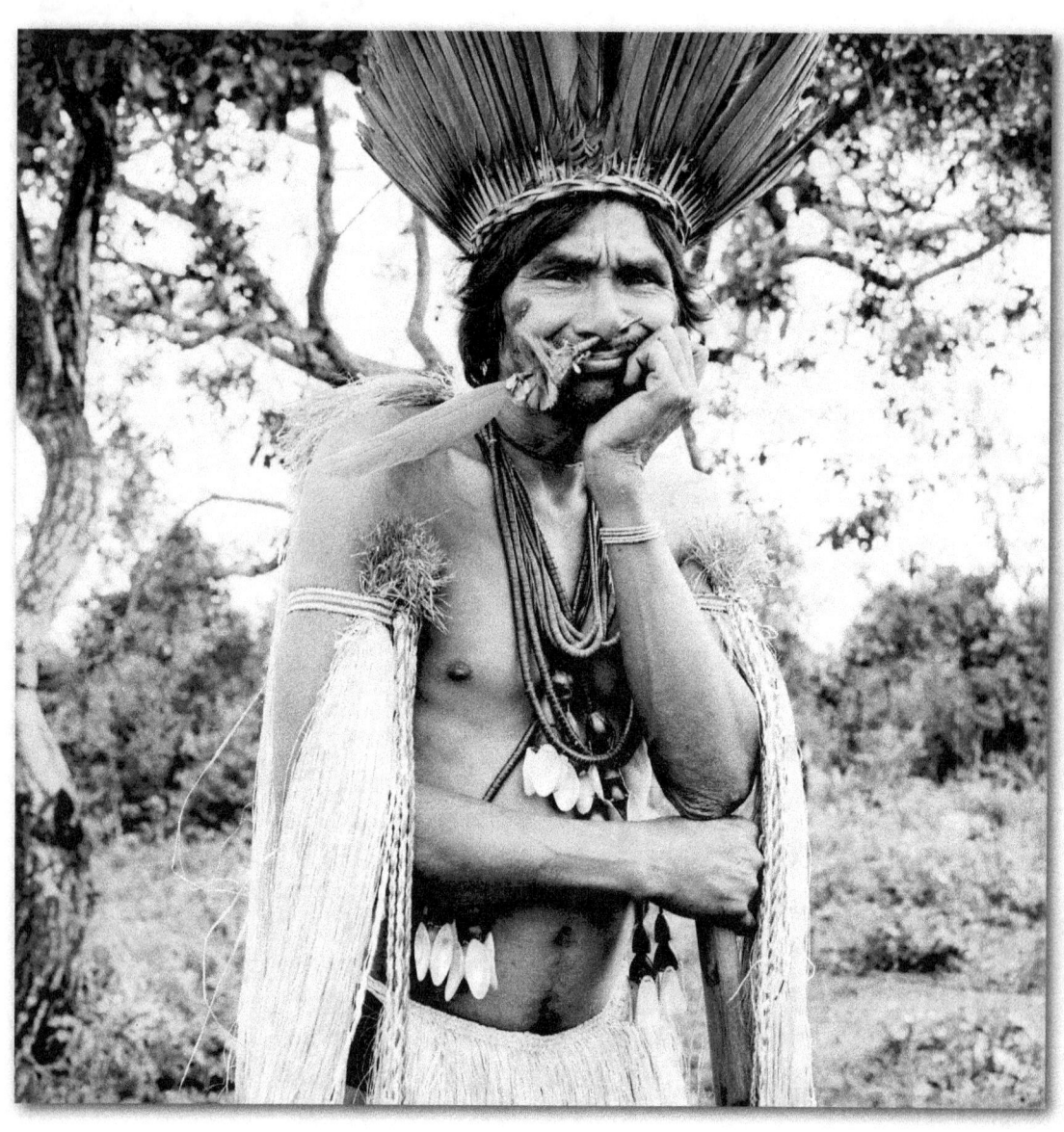

Nambikwara Mamaindê wearing a celebration garment

2008

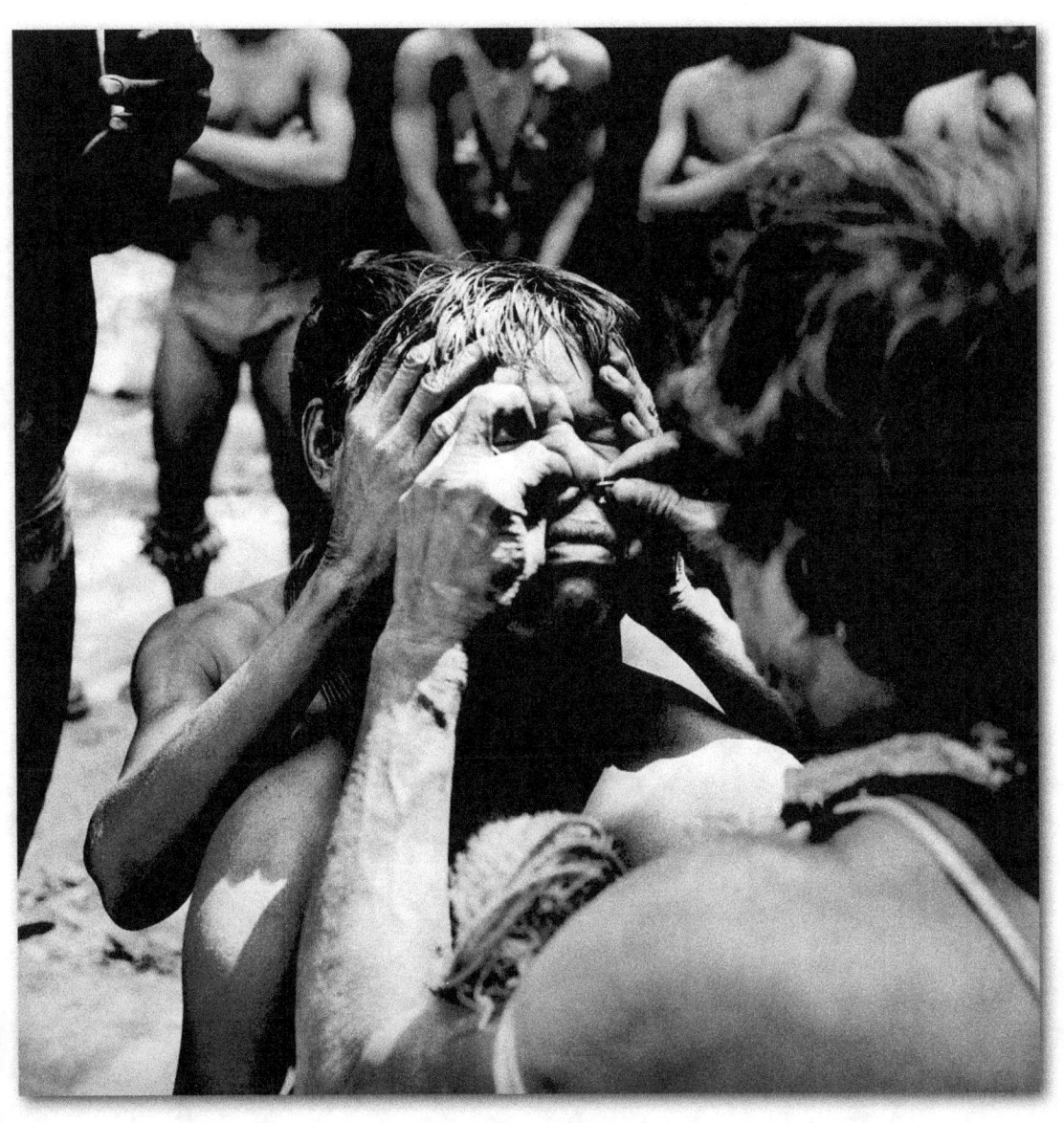

Nose piercing / Men's rite celebration

2008

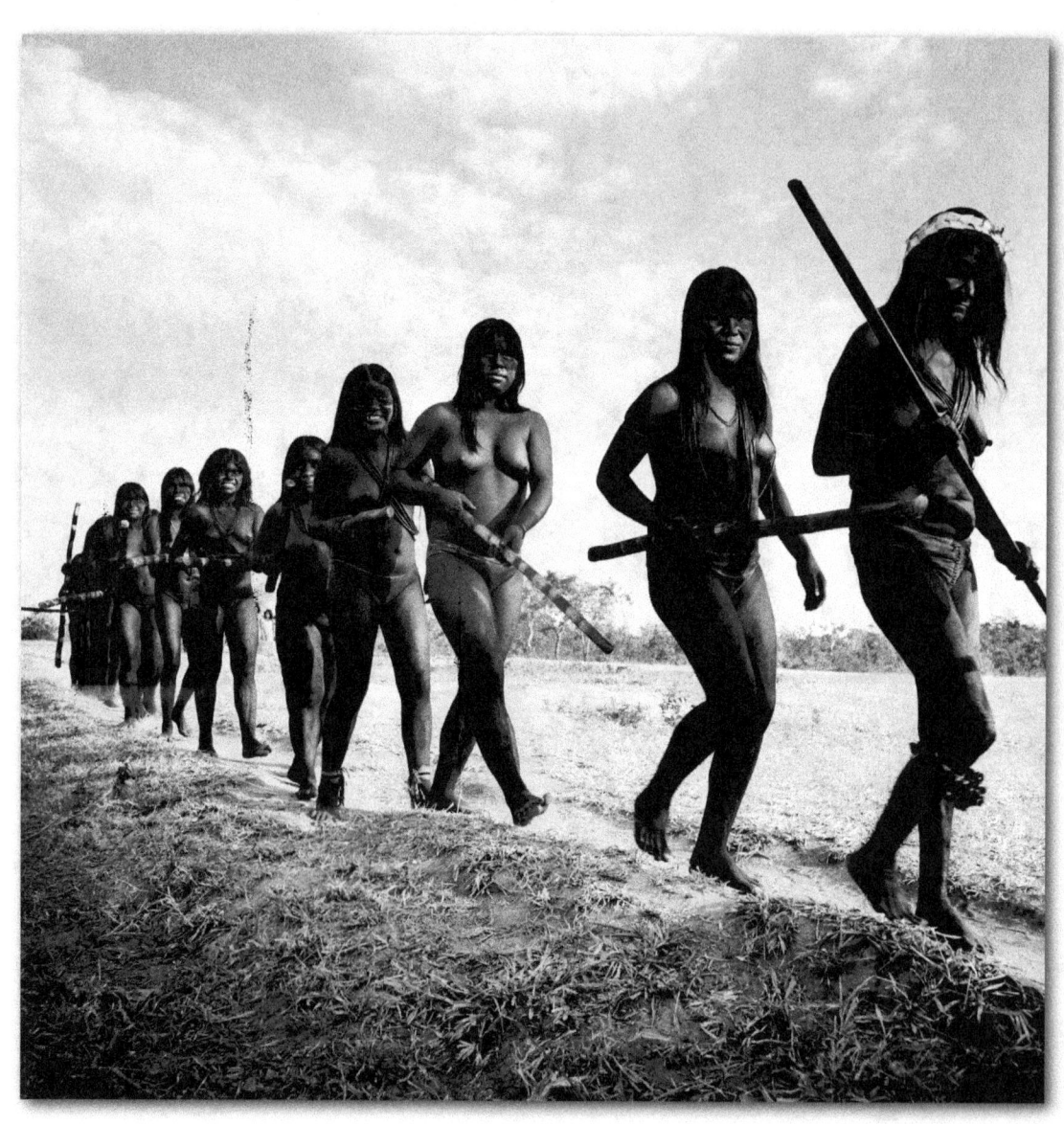

Mamaindê women / War dance invocation

2008

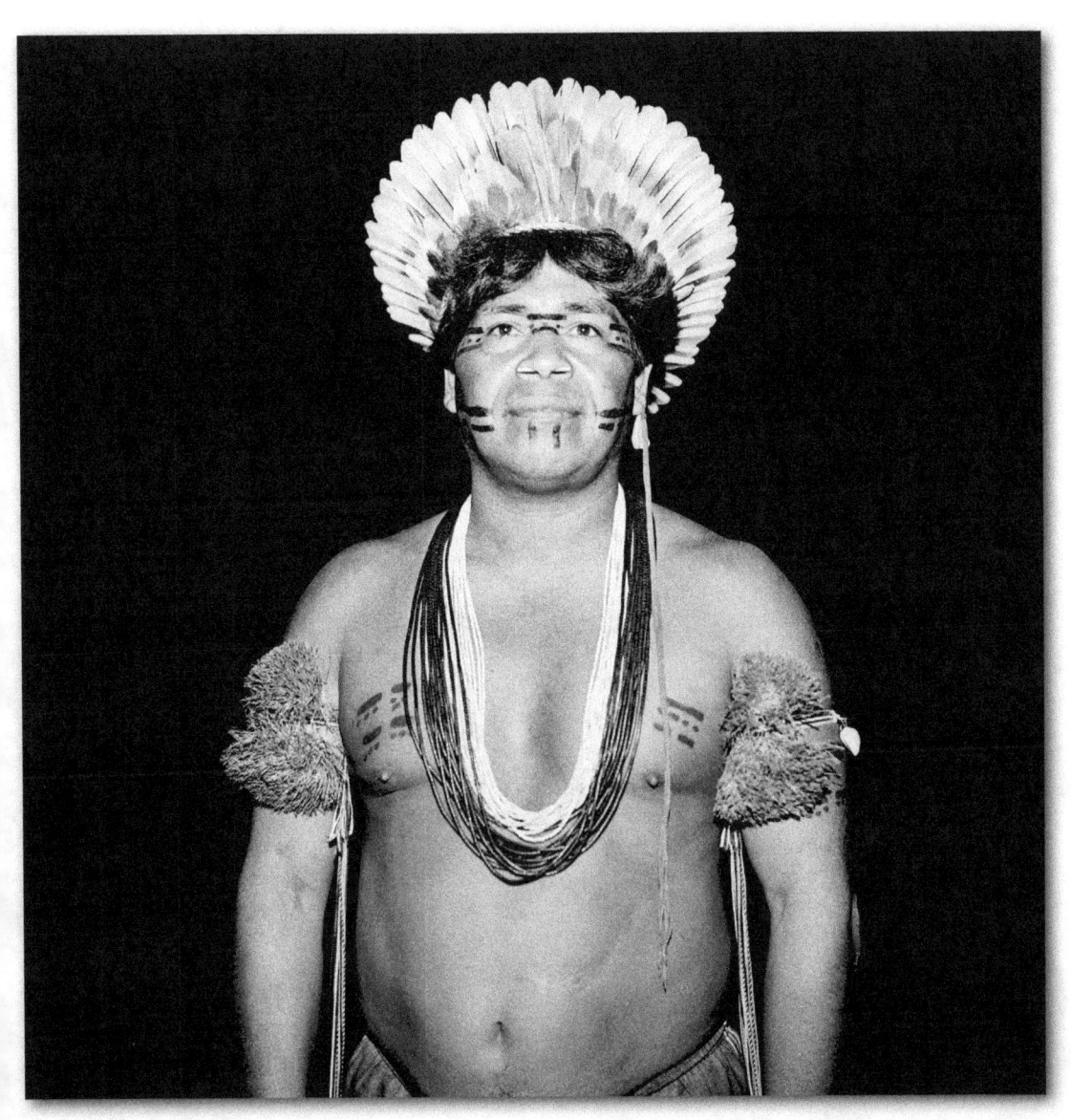

Chief Renato Nambikwara

2005

Krahô

The Krahô, self-styled Mehin, are speakers of a Jê language. Their population is comprised of approximately 3000 individuals living in the northeastern part of Tocantins state, in the Kraholândia Indigenous Land.

I photographed them in April 2007 at the Manuel Alves village, which bears the same name as the river that flows by border of the territory. On this occasion I had the opportunity to photograph the log race, or crowti jaren xà, one of the main Krahô rituals.

The Xavante ethnicity also performs this ritual, sharing some characteristics with the Krahô. In both cases, the race involves participation by two teams —two halves— although with the Krahô these teams are neither unique nor permanent. The Krahô society is constituted of many pairs of halves, which have multiple and changeable matching criteria.

The Krahô became nationally known in 1986 with the reclaiming —and the restitution— of their semilunar stone axe, the kàjre. The sacred object had been taken from Pedra Branca village in 1947, when it was given in exchange of a rifle. The axe was then donated to the Paulista Museum, in São Paulo, by anthropologist Herald Schultz. Almost 40 years later, led by chief Pedro Penon, 11 Krahô arrived in São Paulo to retrieve the axe. After two months of discussions and political obstacles, the University of São Paulo decided to loan the axe to the Krahô indefinitely.

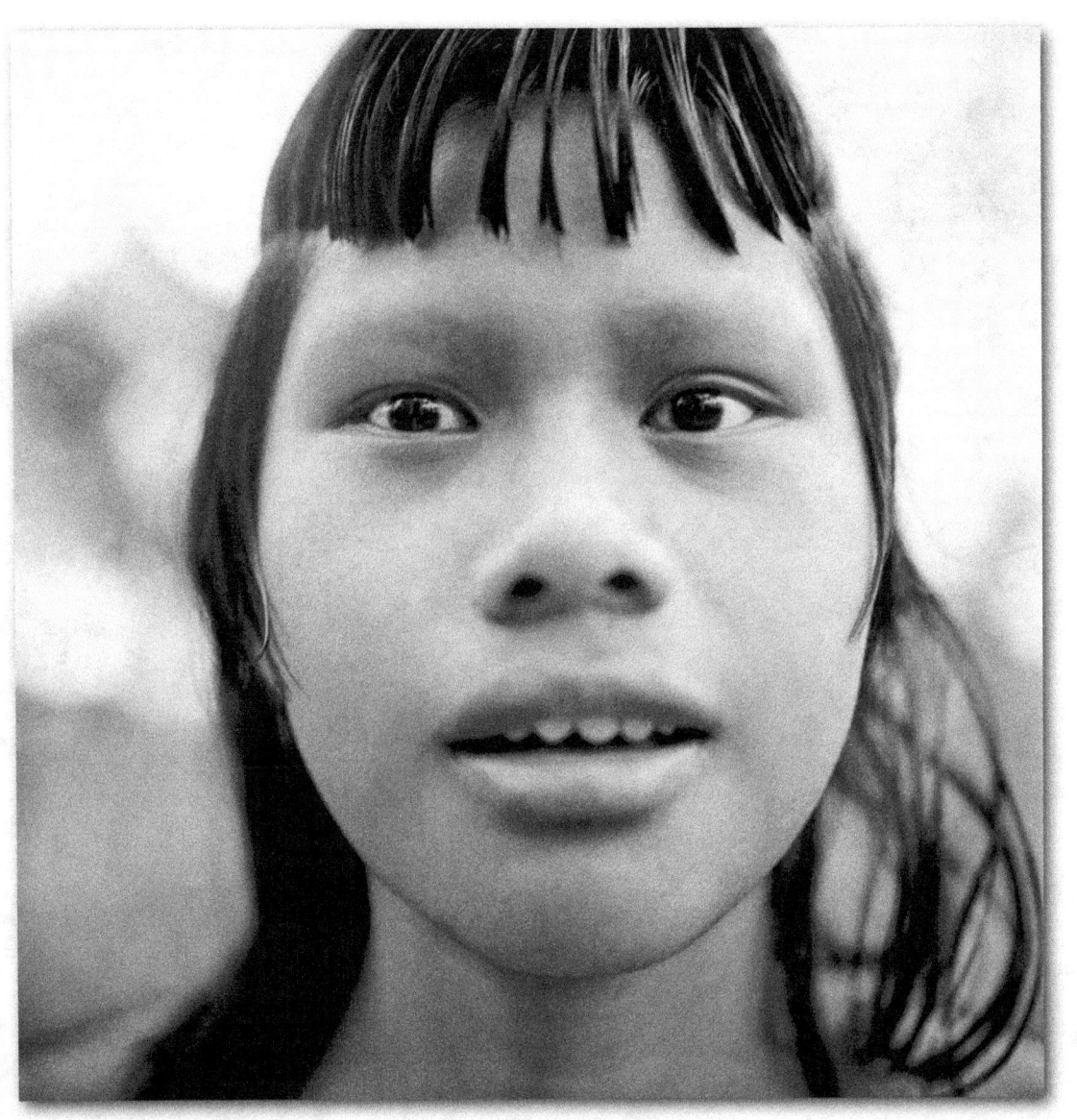

Krahõ / Girl with "piranha tooth"

Tocantins Plains 2006

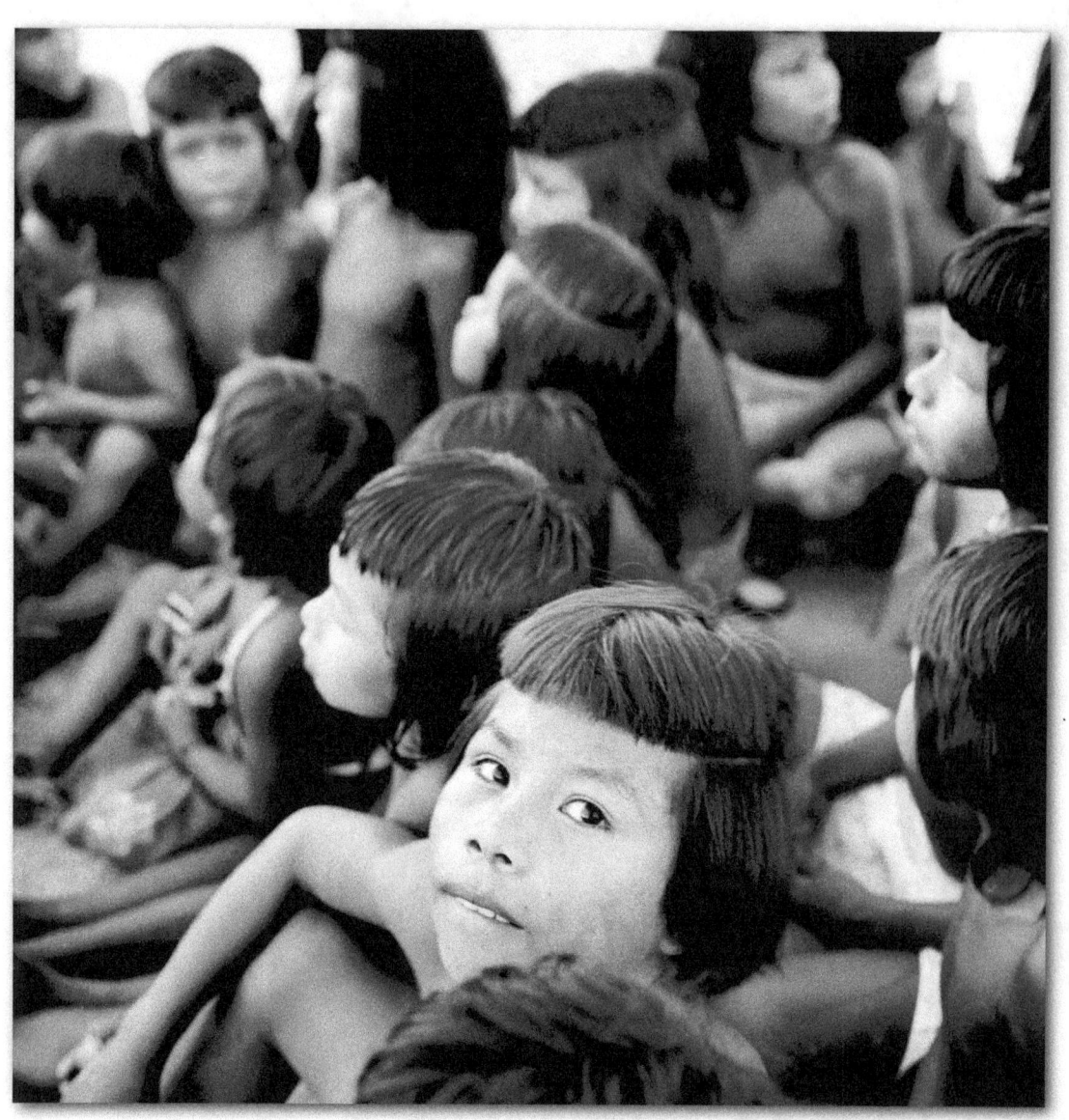

Children paying attention to the Hôxwa (Crown like figure)

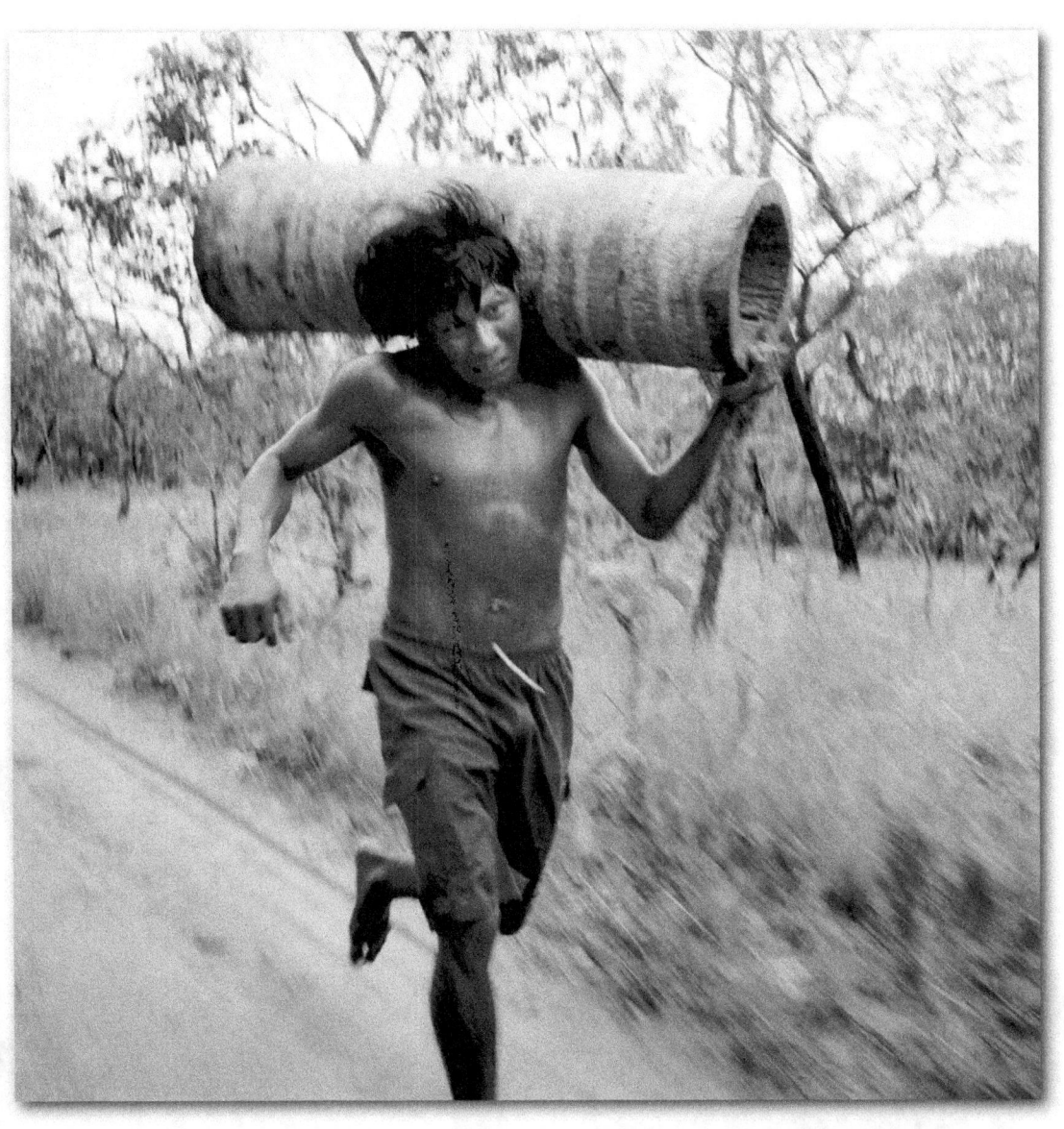

Log race (Crowti jaren xà) at the Potato celebration (Jàt jõ pî)

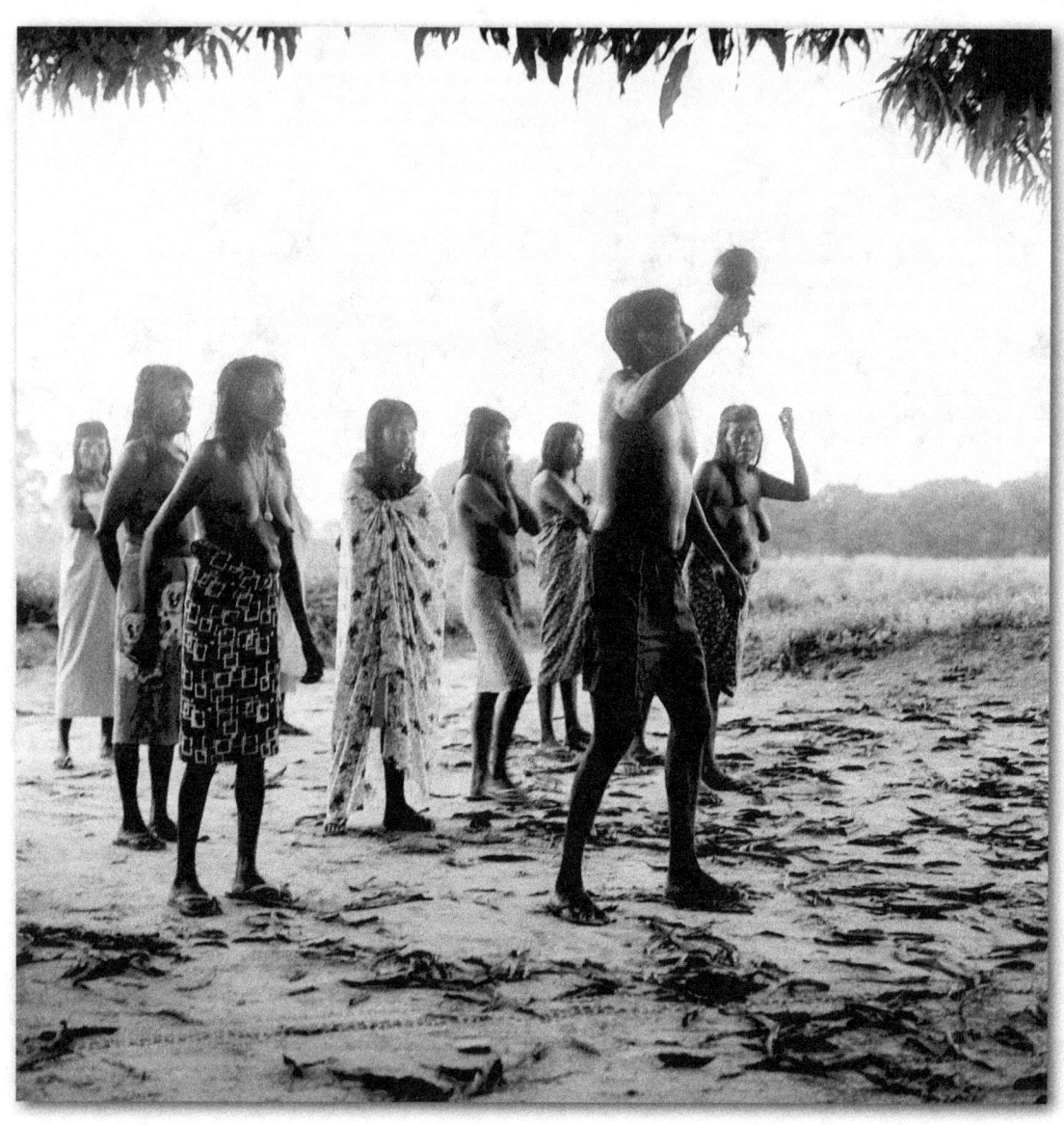

Osmar Cuhkõ Krahõ / Singer

2006

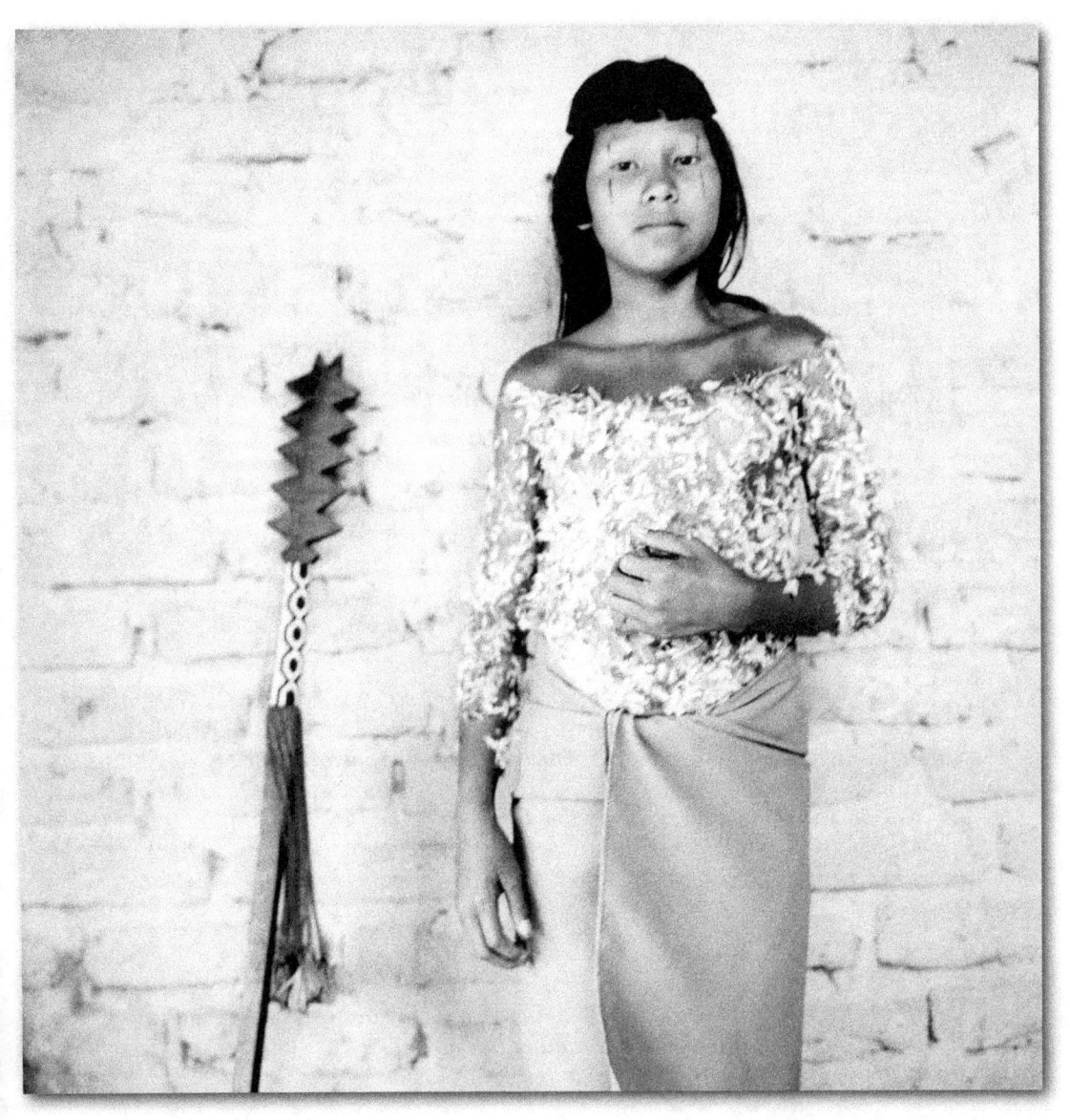

Krahõ / Girl with body empennage

2006

Envira

In November 2004, after being invited by local leaders, I took a 9-day boat trip on the Envira River, sailing from Feijó, Acré, almost to the Peruvian border. The 512-kilometer long river flows from the Andes, crossing the state of Acre until reaching the town of Envira, Amazonas. Today, the river and the indigenous people living by the riverside suffer the effects of the drug trafficking routes in the region.

There are eight indigenous territories alongside the Envira, which are occupied by different ethnicities such as the Kawashiná (self-styled Huni Kuin), Ashaninka, Shenenáwa, Kulina Madijá and other isolated peoples. The following pages present a selection of images divided in two parts: the Kashinawá and the Ashaninka, despite the presence of a few Kulina Madijá among them.

I was lucky to arrive at a village on the day before the fertility ritual, or katxanawa, also known as mariri. During this ritual, yuxin (spirits) of fertility are summoned, so that they might help ensure the abundance of food and life at the village. I would not have been able to photograph the ritual if it weren't for the Kashinawá's understanding, since I had to ask them to wait until the morning so there would be enough light to take the photos.

With the Ashaninka, who we see wearing their elegant cusmas, something curious happened. I arrived at a village next to the Peruvian border, just before nightfall. They invited me to a ball, a forró, to which almost all the village inhabitants would attend. That is how I photographed this couple, dancing all through the night with their little child in their arms.

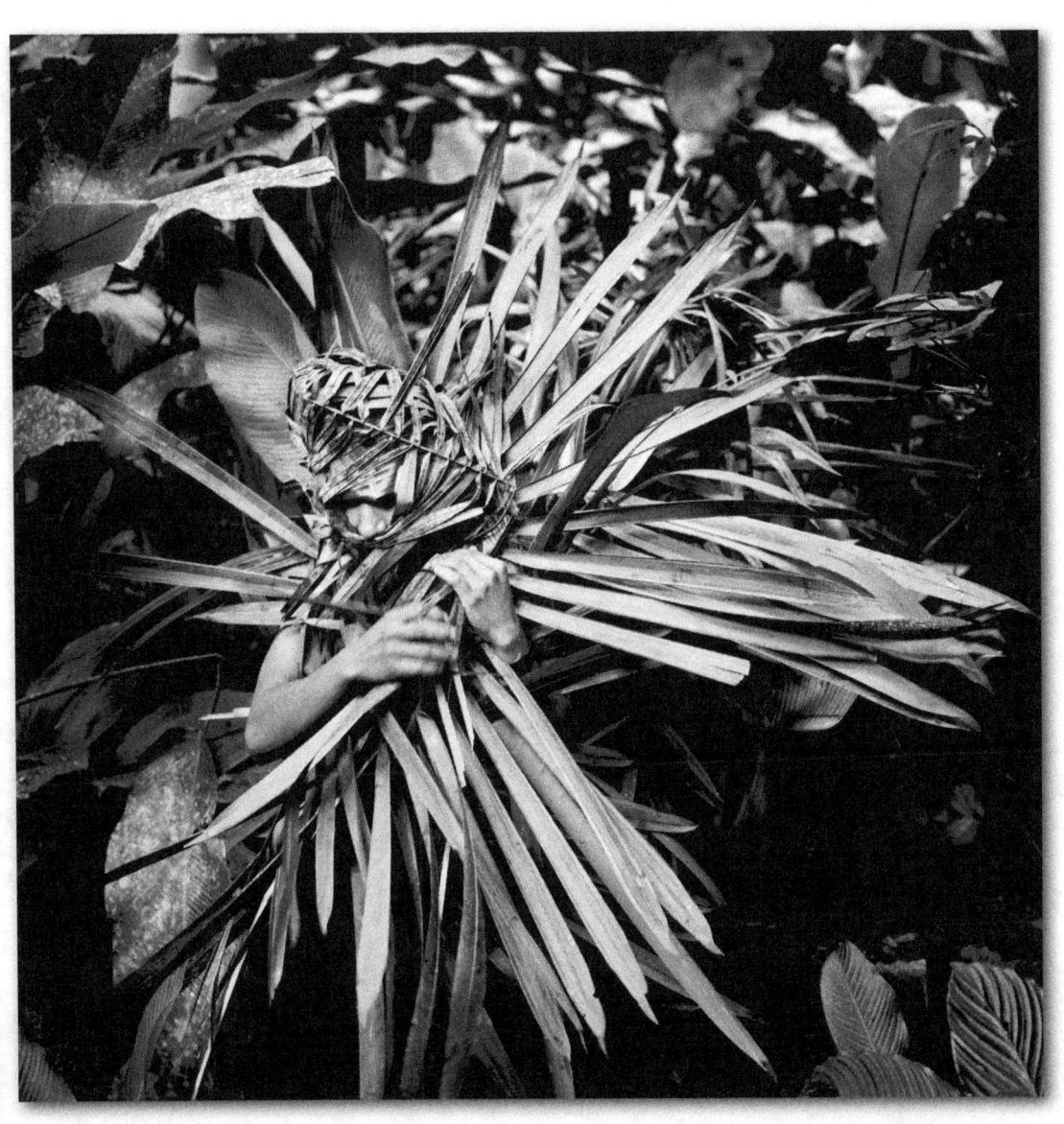

Kashinawá / In preparation to recevi the Yuxin (spirits)

Alto Envira river / Acre 2004

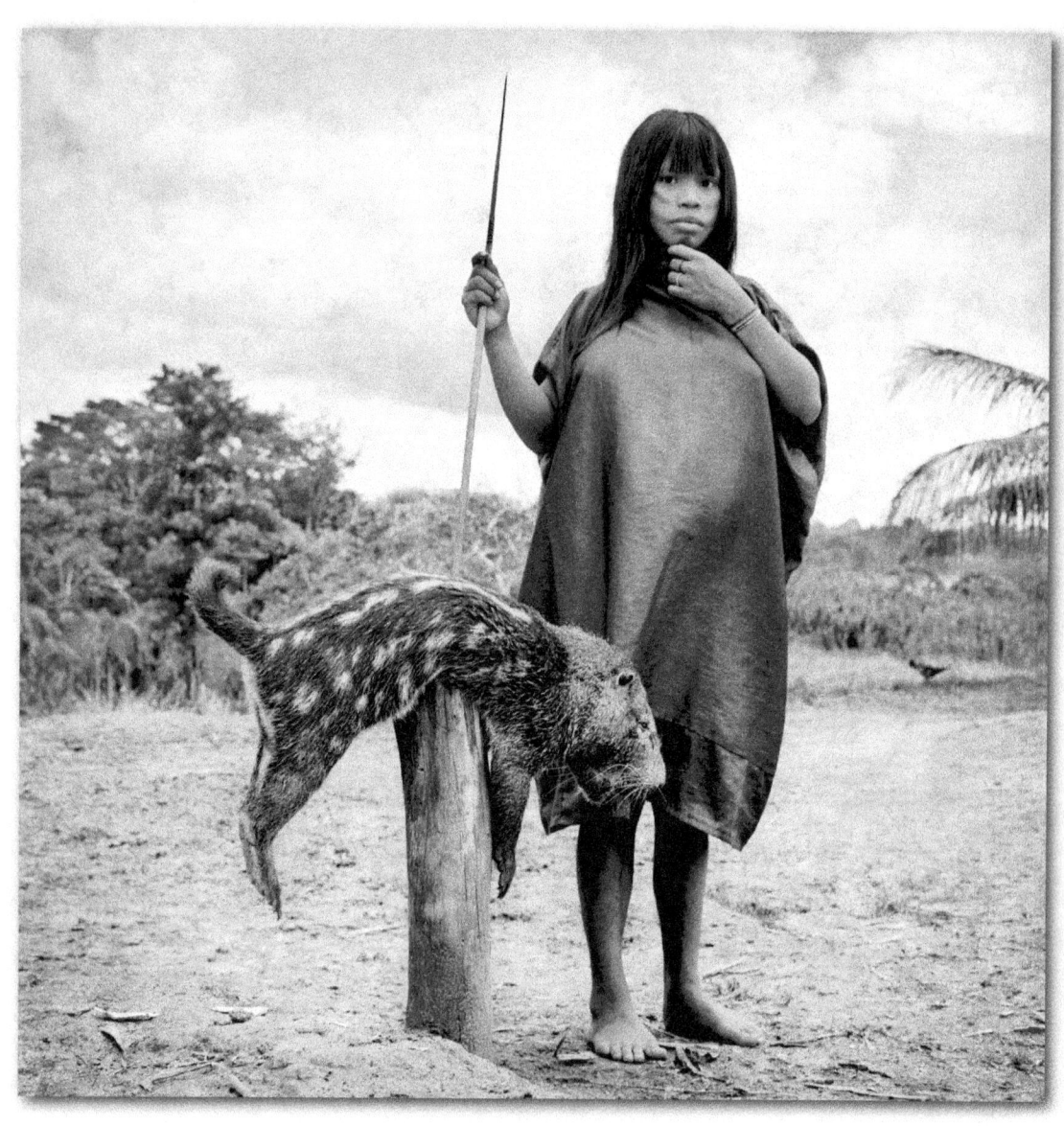

Kulina-Madihá / Girl with Pacarana (Dinomys branickii)

2004

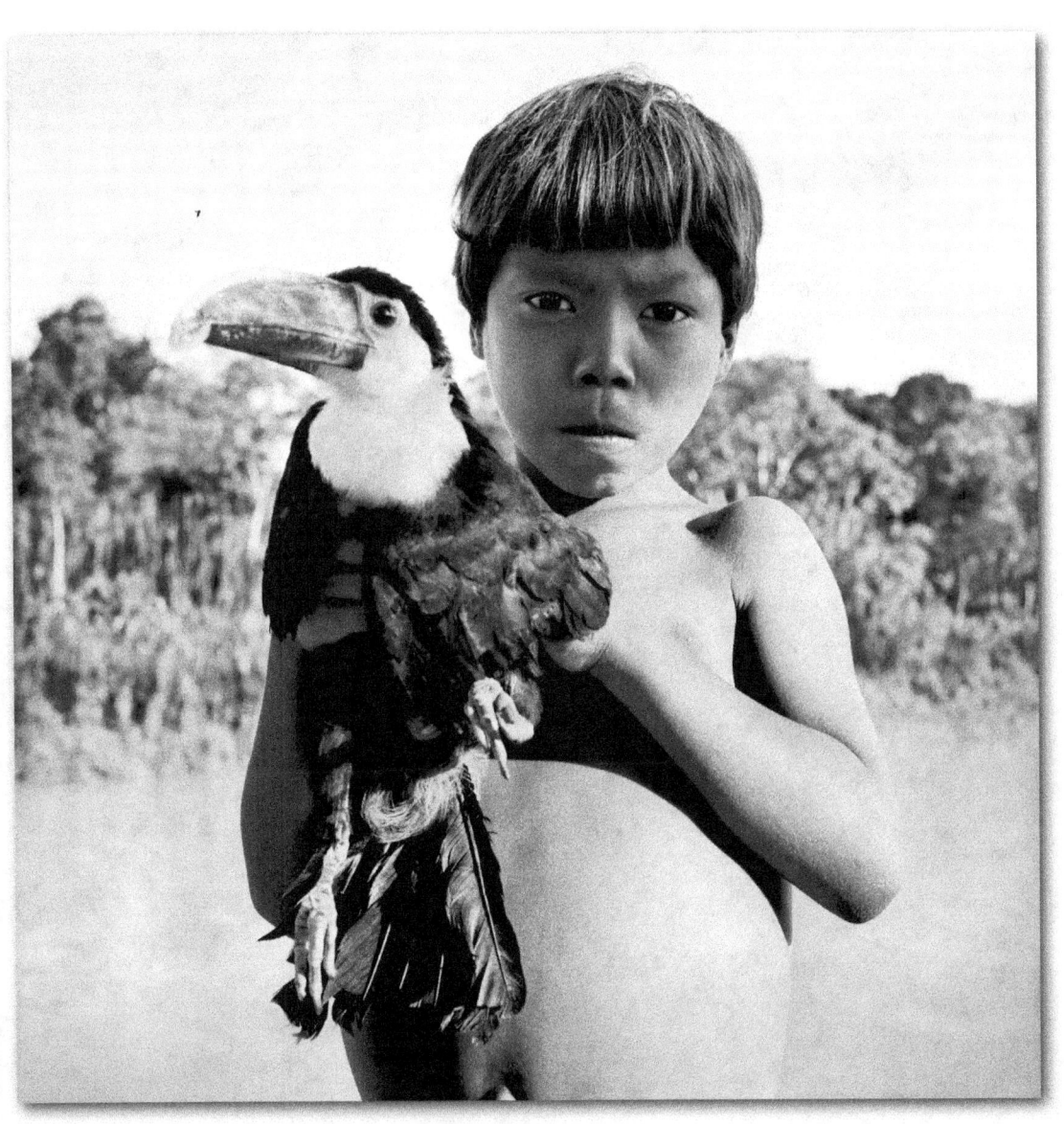

Kulina -Madihá / Boy with toucan (genus Rhamphastos)

2004

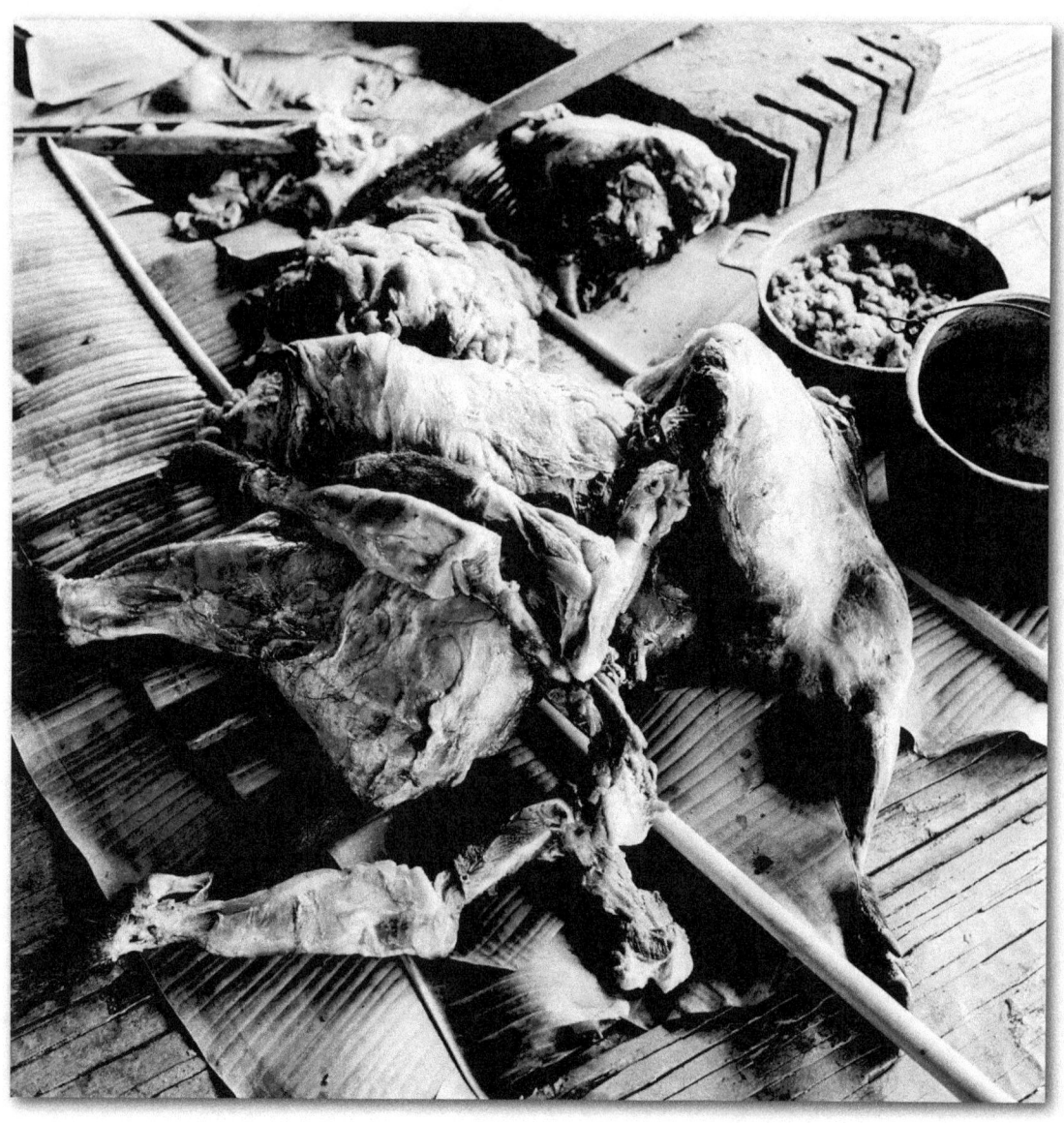

Smoked Dear with side dishes over banana leafs

2004

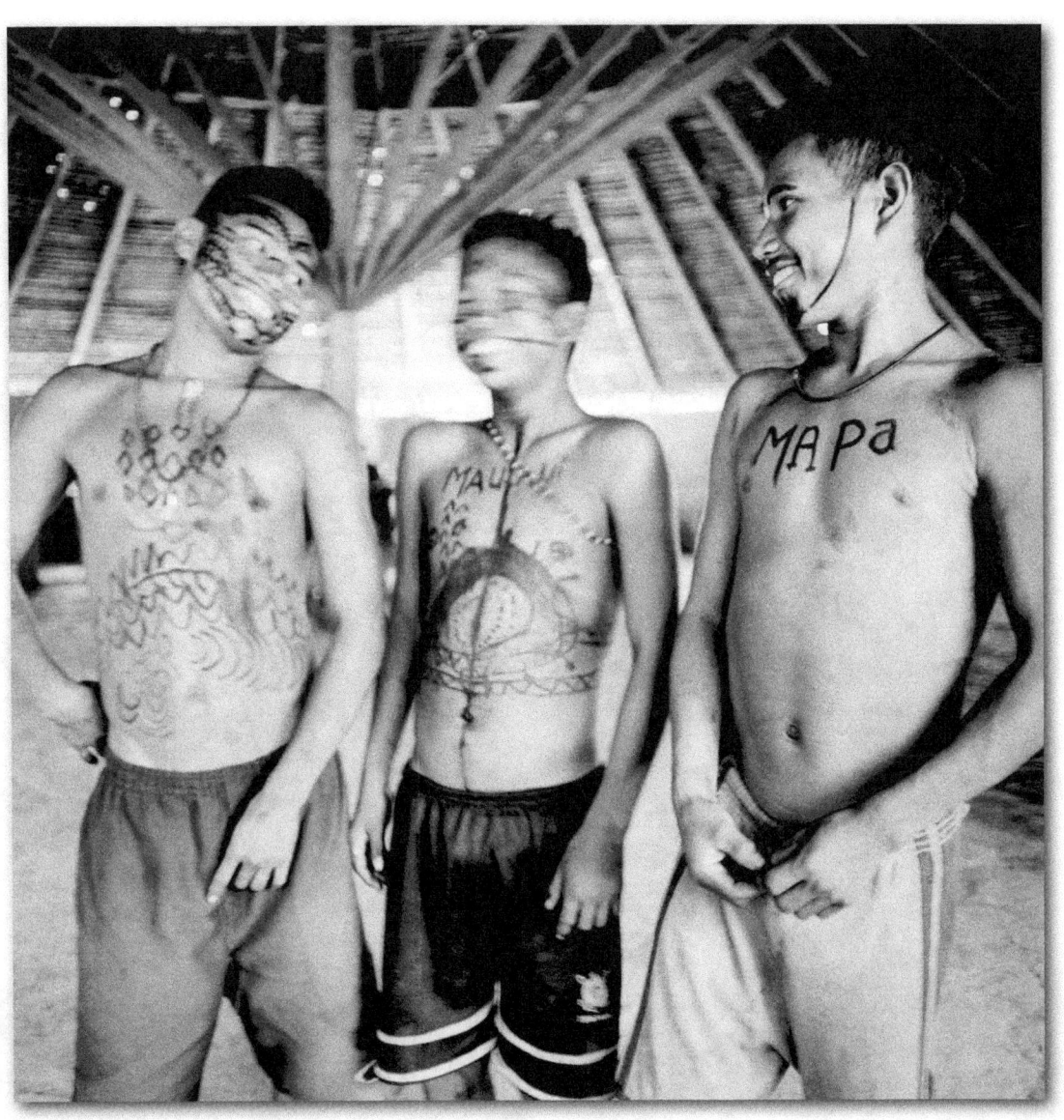

Morada Nova community / Celebration among different ethnicities

circa Feijó 2004

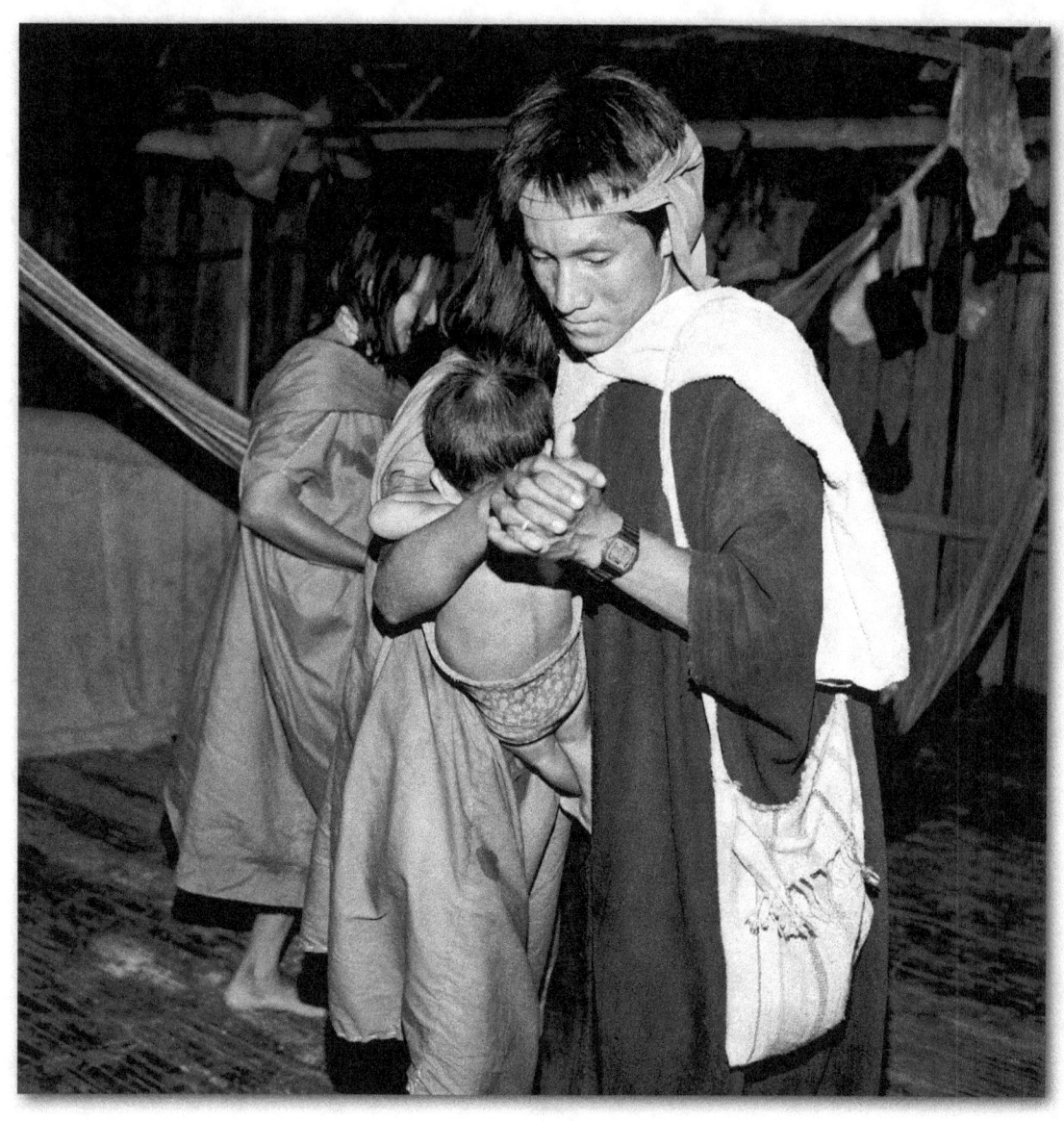

Ashaninka father, mother and child / Forró dance late at night

2004

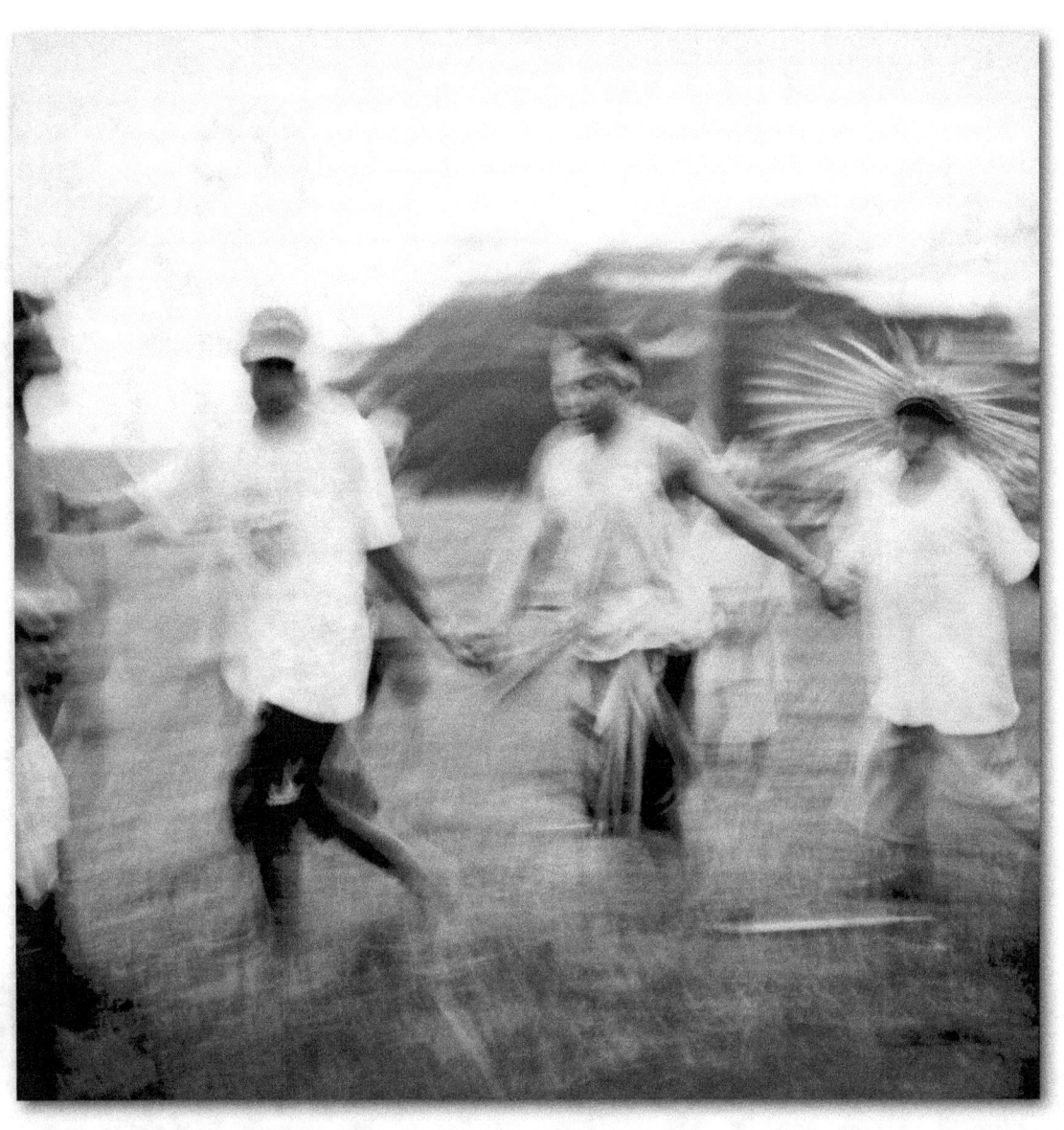

Kashinawa / Welcome celebration before sunset

2004

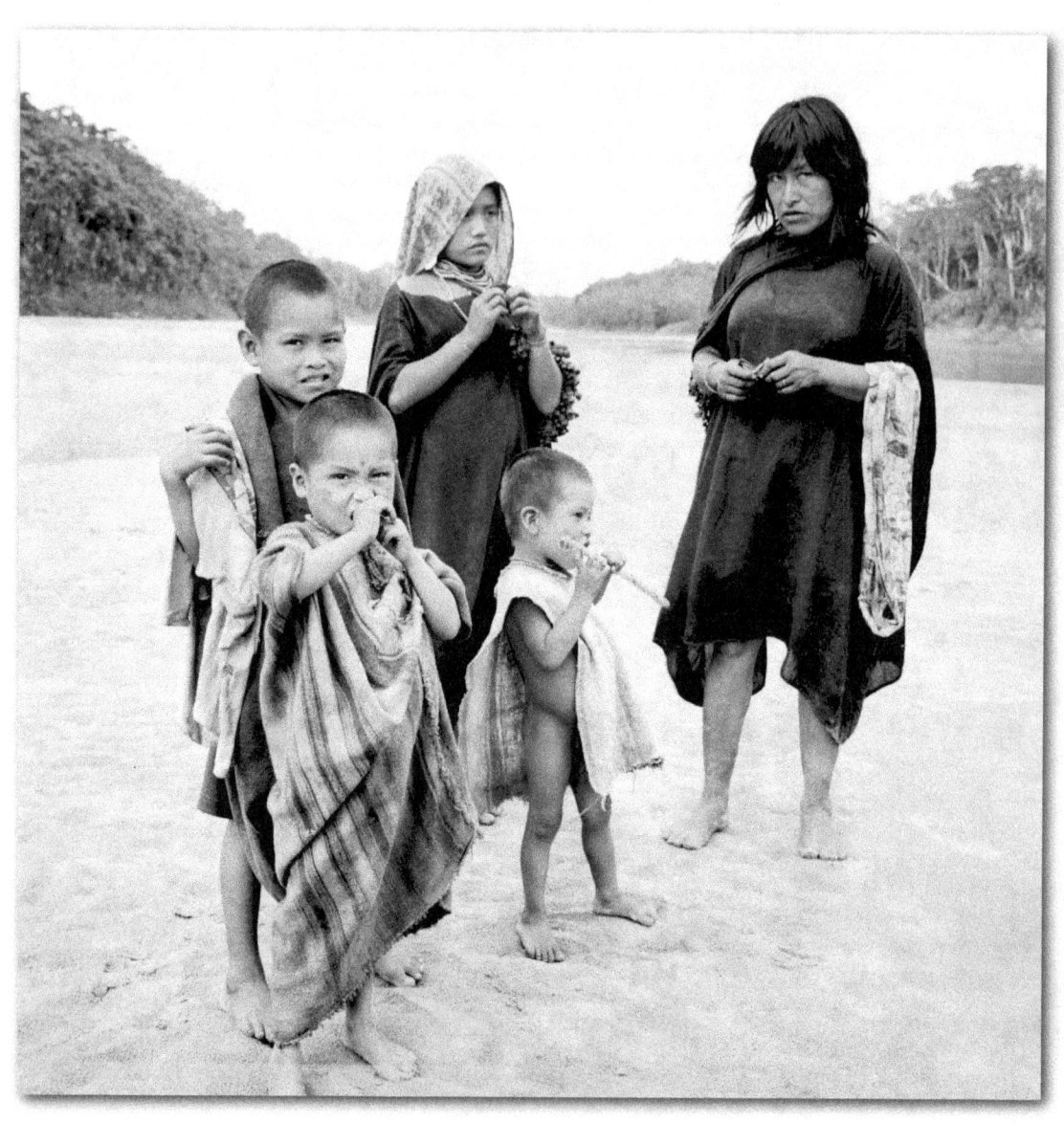

Ashaninka / Mother and children at river bottoms

2004

Rikbaktsa

The Rikbatsá lands spread through Mato Grosso state, divided in three indigenous lands demarcated by the Federal Government - Rikbaktsá, Japuíra and Escondido - all three by the banks of Juruena river. 102 hydropower plants are expected to be built on the Tapajós river basin, six of them on the Juruena river, causing damage to the rivers and many of the lives that depend upon them, leaving a huge impact upon the population and the environment.

Today the Rikbaktsá are comprised of approximately 2000 people, speakers of a Macro-Jê language. Around 75% of their population died after the first years of contact with non-indigenous people between 1942 and 1957, due to their vulnerability against diseases such as the flu, having been reduced to as few as 300 people during this time period.

Their beautifully skilled feather work is a distinguishing characteristic of their culture. In view of the growing demand for consumer goods and with the prohibition of feather work commercialization by the Brazilian Institute of the Environment and Renewable Natural Resources (IBAMA), the Rikbaktsá have been looking for new sources of income, such as the trading of rubber, nuts and feather-free handicraft.

The Rikbaktsá are also known not only for their canoeing skills but also for the wooden disks worn in their ear lobes. Some examples of these can be seen in some of the pictures that I took in October 2003 at the Curva village, next to the town of Fontanilhas, Mato Grosso state

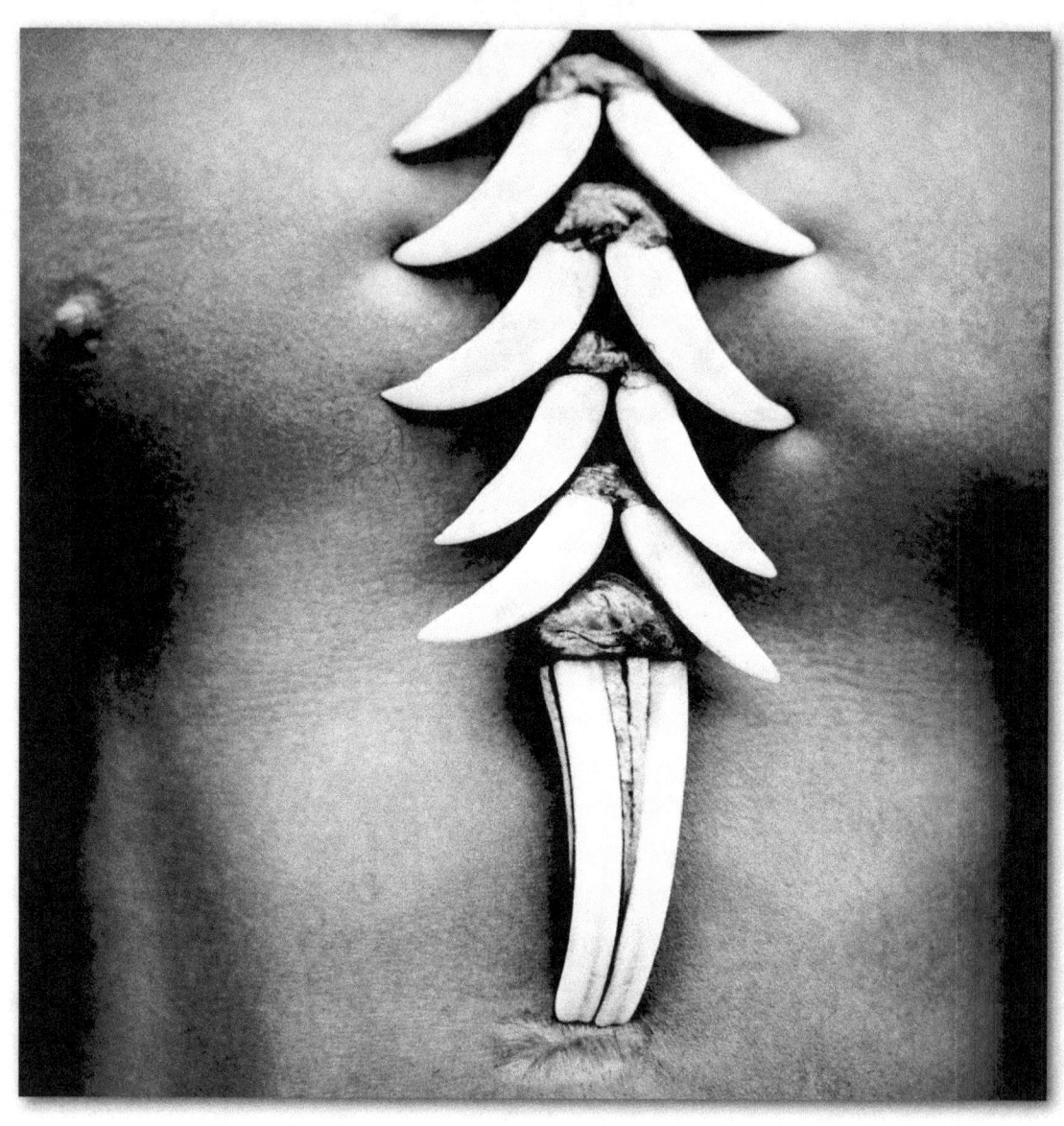

Rikbaktsa / Men's necklace (Itsodikewytsa)

Pé-de-Mutum community - Mato Grosso 2004

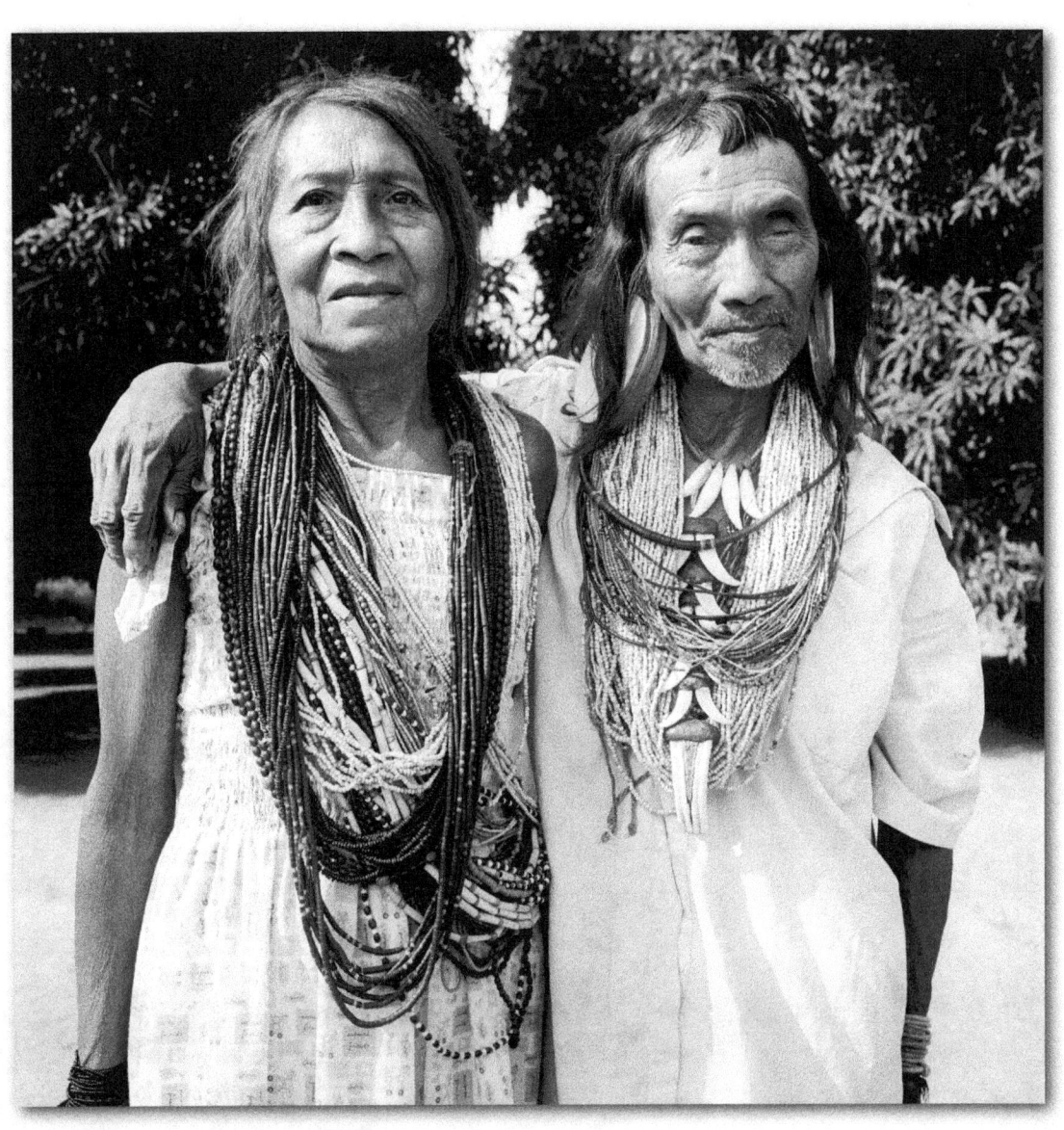

Geraldino Muitsy Rikbaktsa & wife (Makwaraktsa Clan)

Curva community- 2003

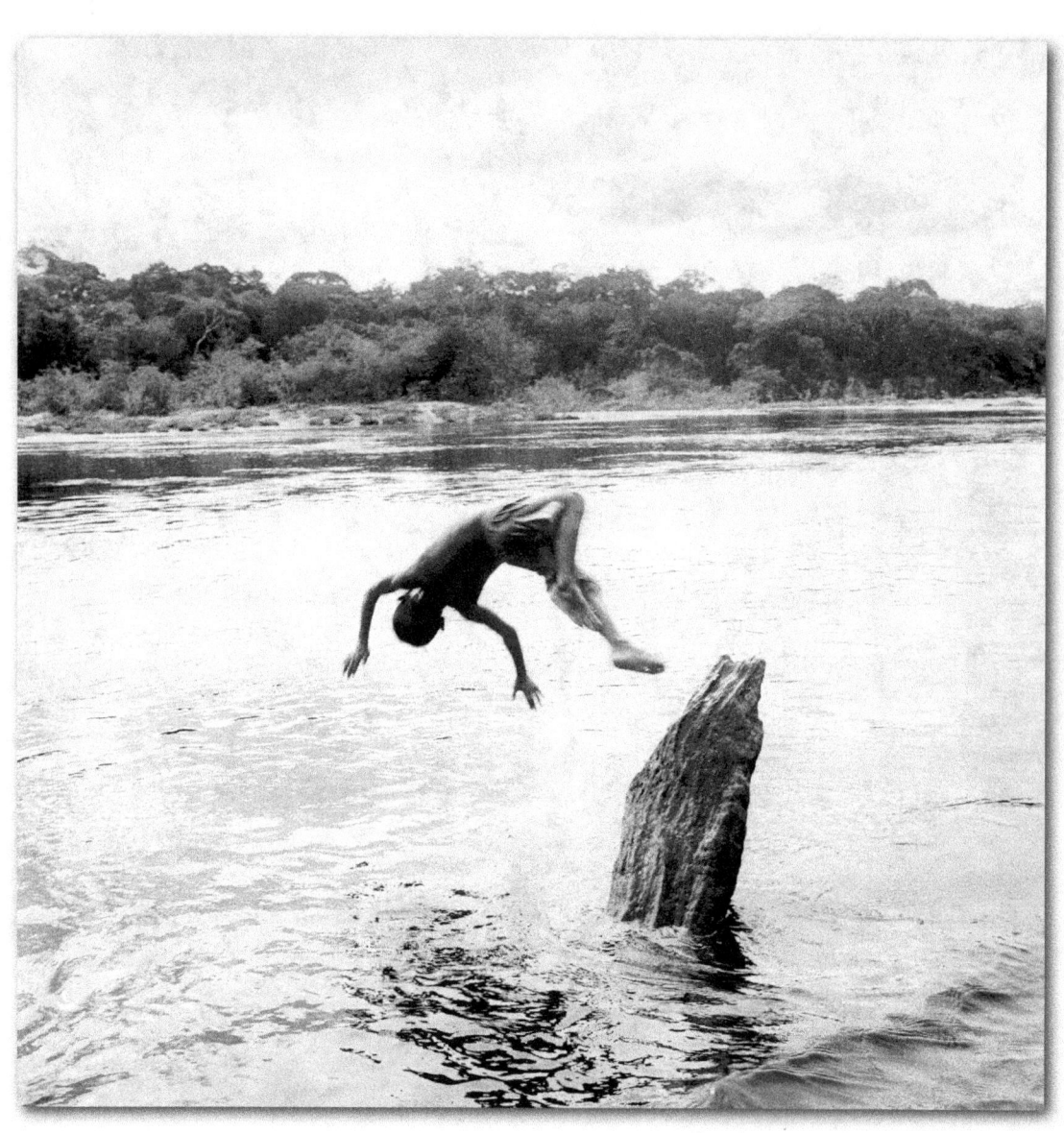

Juruena River

circa Fontanilhas city - 2003

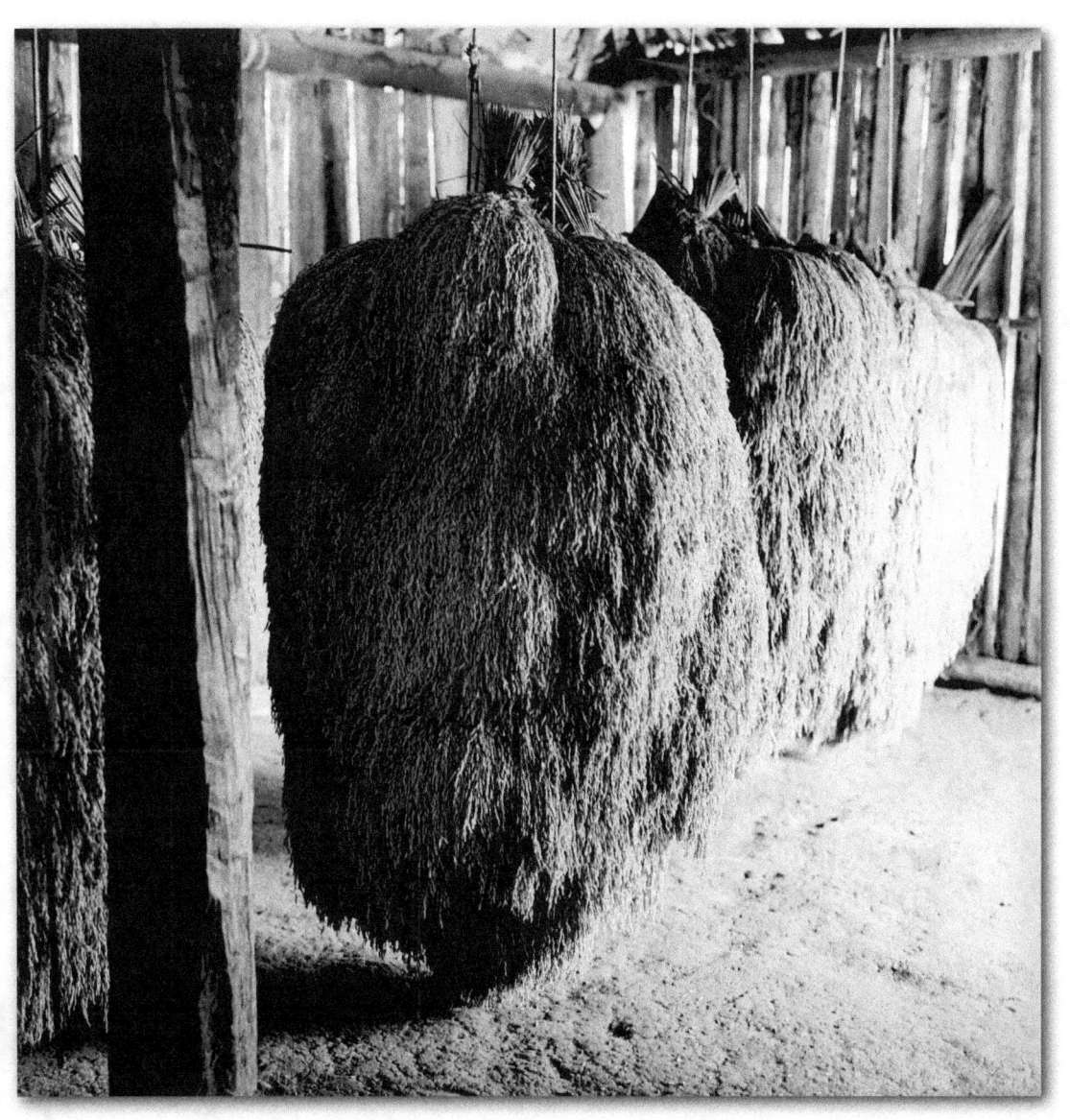

Rice stack (Round log bar)

2003

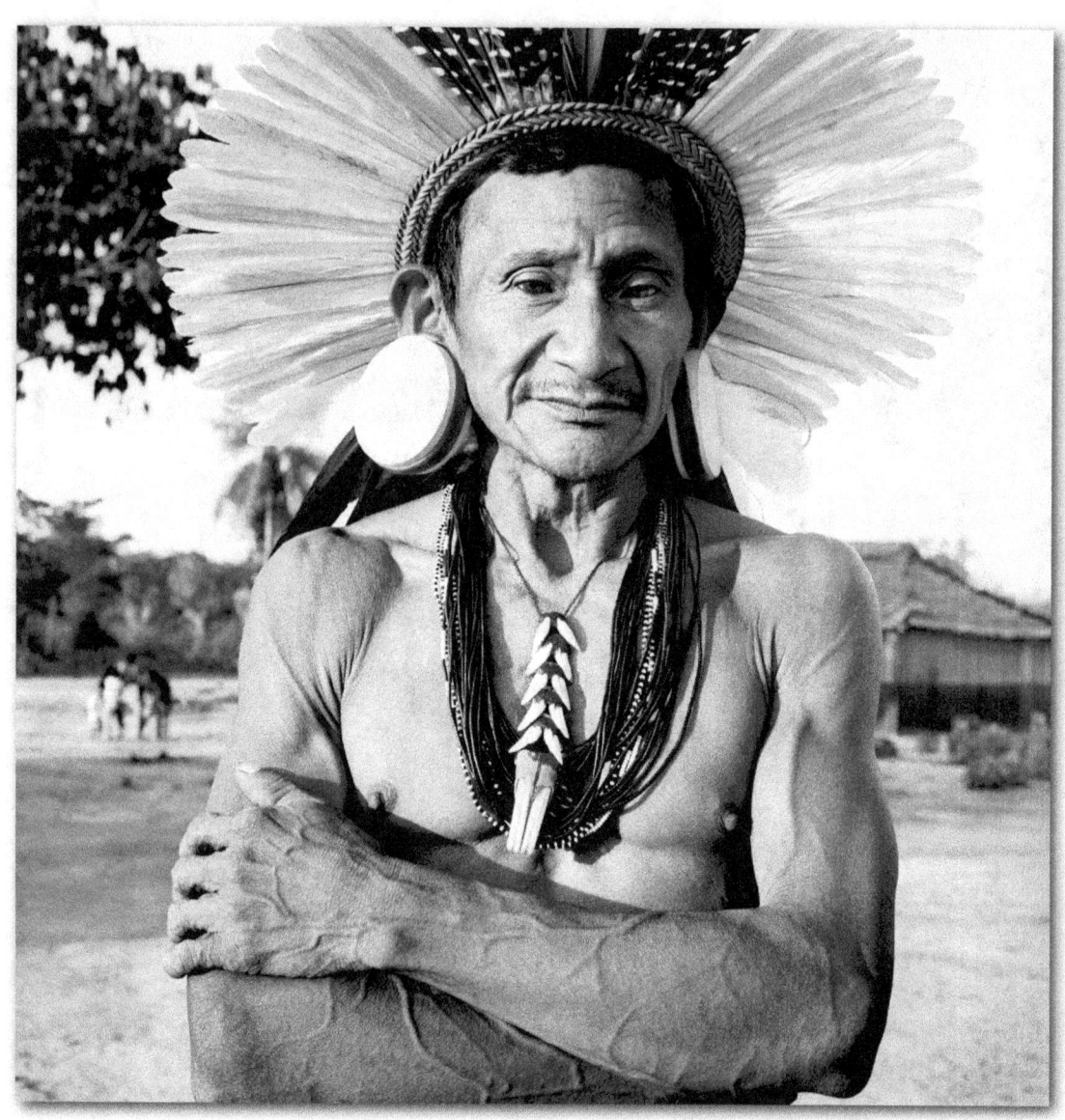

Rikbaktsa / Hawk feather headdress (Iwohorekpakezi)

2003

Enawenê-Nawê

The Enawenê-Nawê live in a single village named Halataikwa. They are comprised of approximately 700 people divided into 10 clans, which count amongst their ranks not only people, but also subterranean and celestial spirits related to flute groups and descendants of mythical populations that came out of stones and spread through the region. They speak an Aruak language and live in the northwest region of Matogrosso state.

The first official contact with the non-indigenous society occurred in 1974 with Jesuits. The village is arranged in a circle of communal rectangular houses (hakolo). In the center of the circle is the house of flutes, called yaokwa hakolo. Yaokwa is also the name of the ritual that is of key importance to the Enawenê's social and cosmological maintenance.

The ritual, that takes seven months to complete, is performed with the exchange of food between the Enawenê-Nawê and the subterranean spirits (iakayreti) who were doomed to live in eternal hunger, depending on the Enawenê-Nawê to be fed with fish and vegetable salt. Due to the ritual complexity and the long duration, the Enawenê-Nawê build the waiti, wooden barriers made of logs tied with vines, which are placed on the river waters and thus allowing an abundance of fishing.

These photographs, taken between March and September 2008, are the record of one of the last structures built by the Enawenê-Nawê. With increasing deforestation, predatory fishing and the proliferation of hydropower plants on the Juruena river, the fish population has decreased, forcing them to search for new food sources.

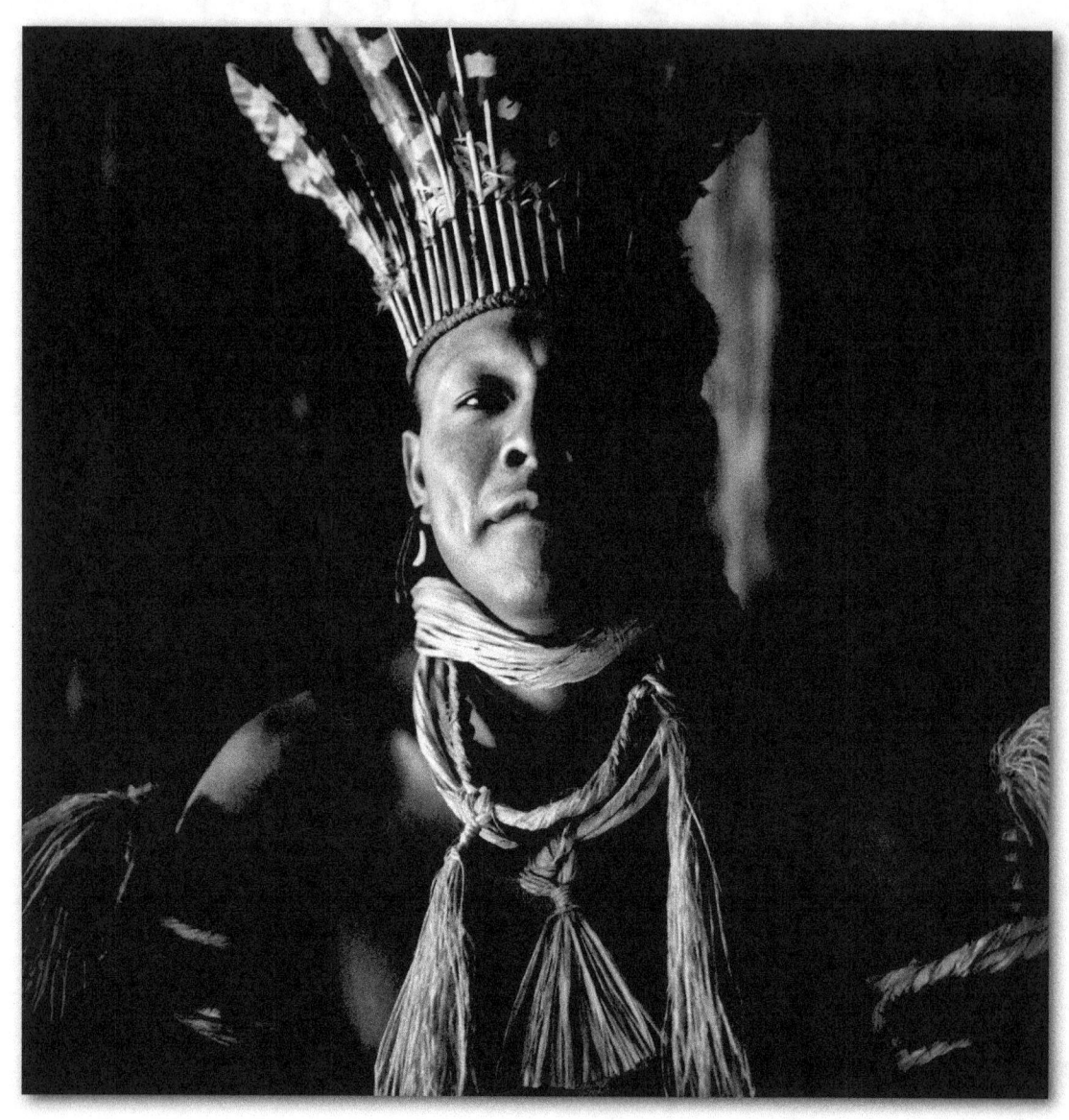

Enawenê-Nawê / Halataikwa community

2008

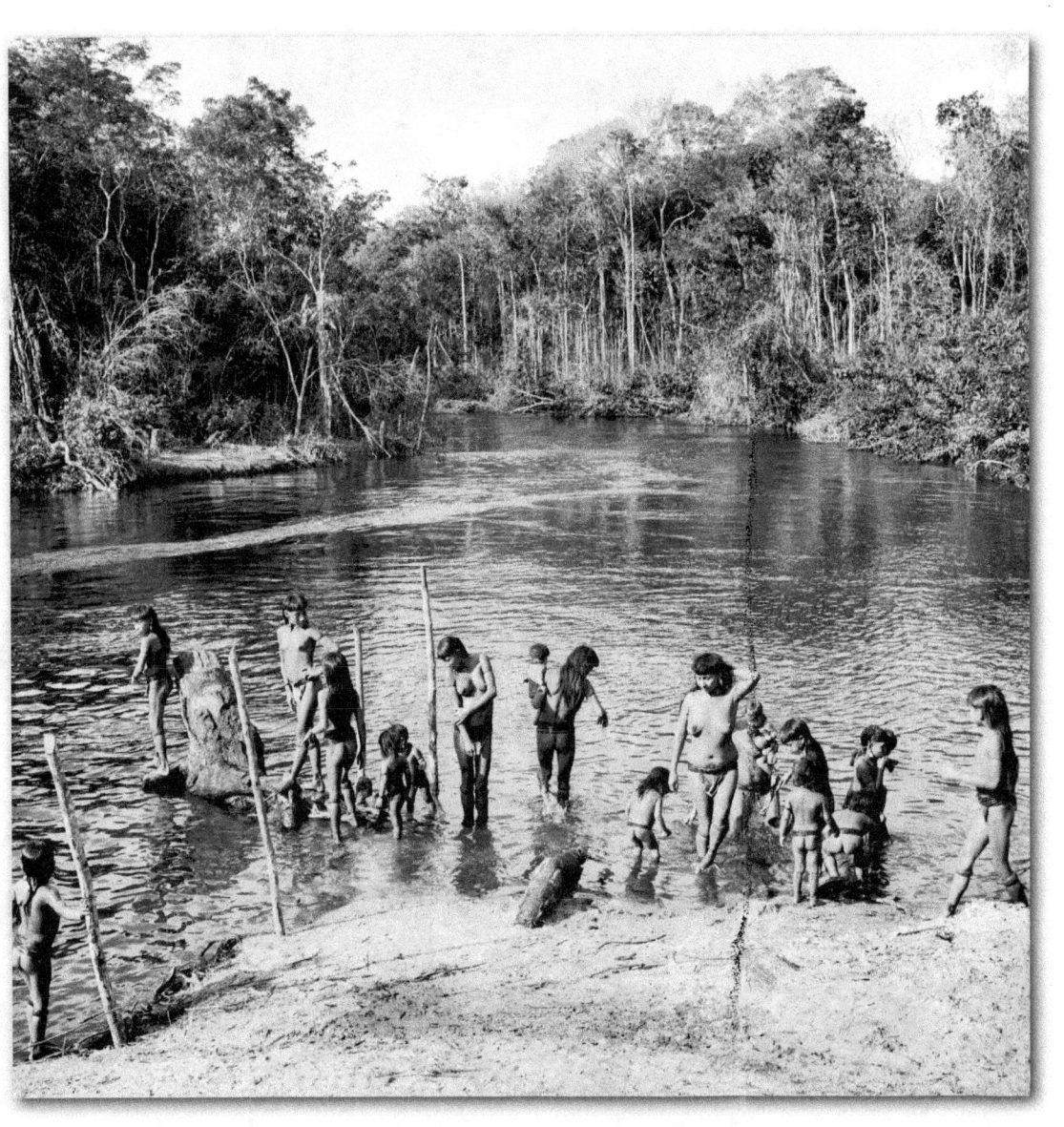

Women's river bath / Late afternoon at Iquê river

2008

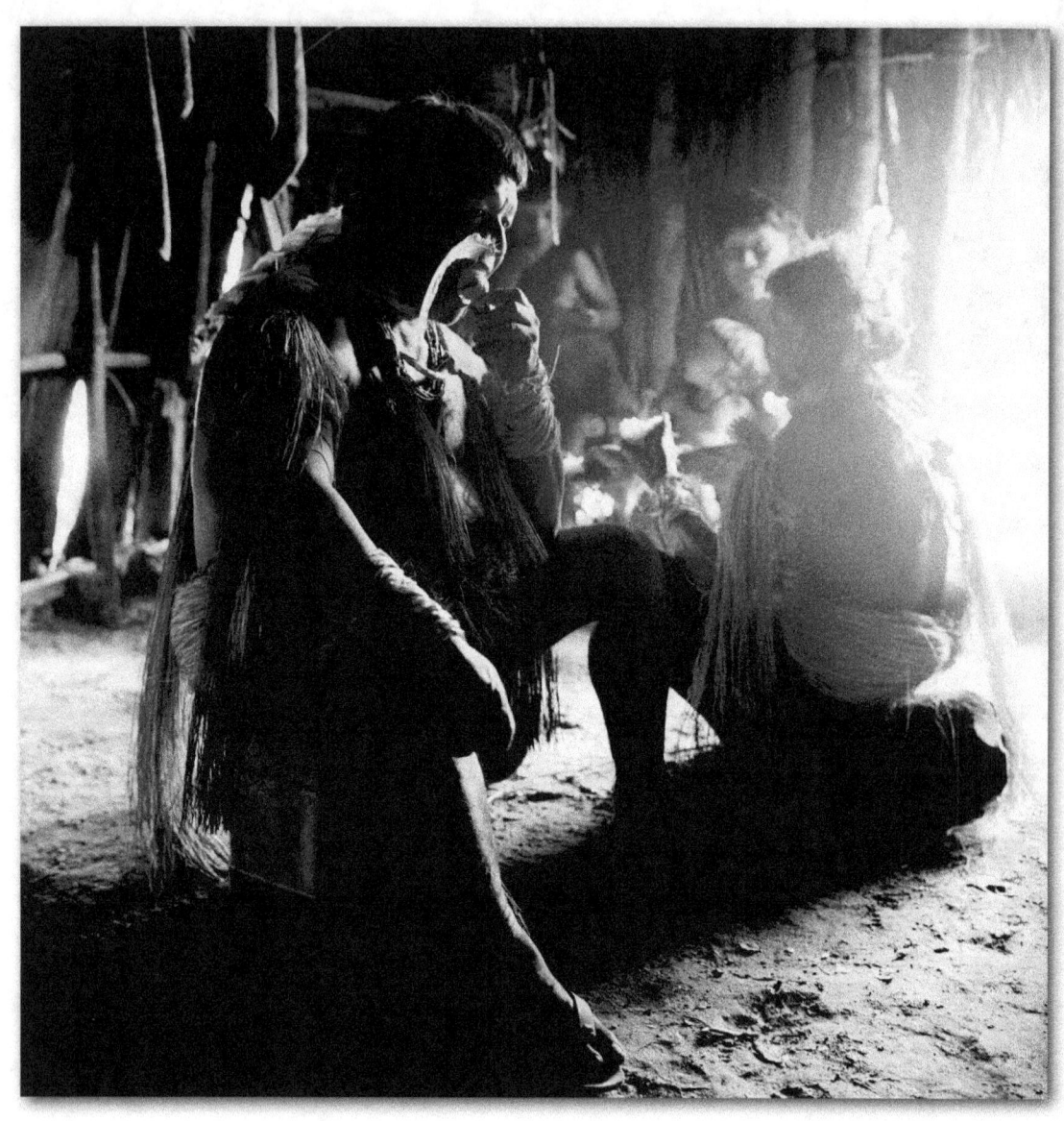

Lunch time inside the communal house (hakolo)

2008

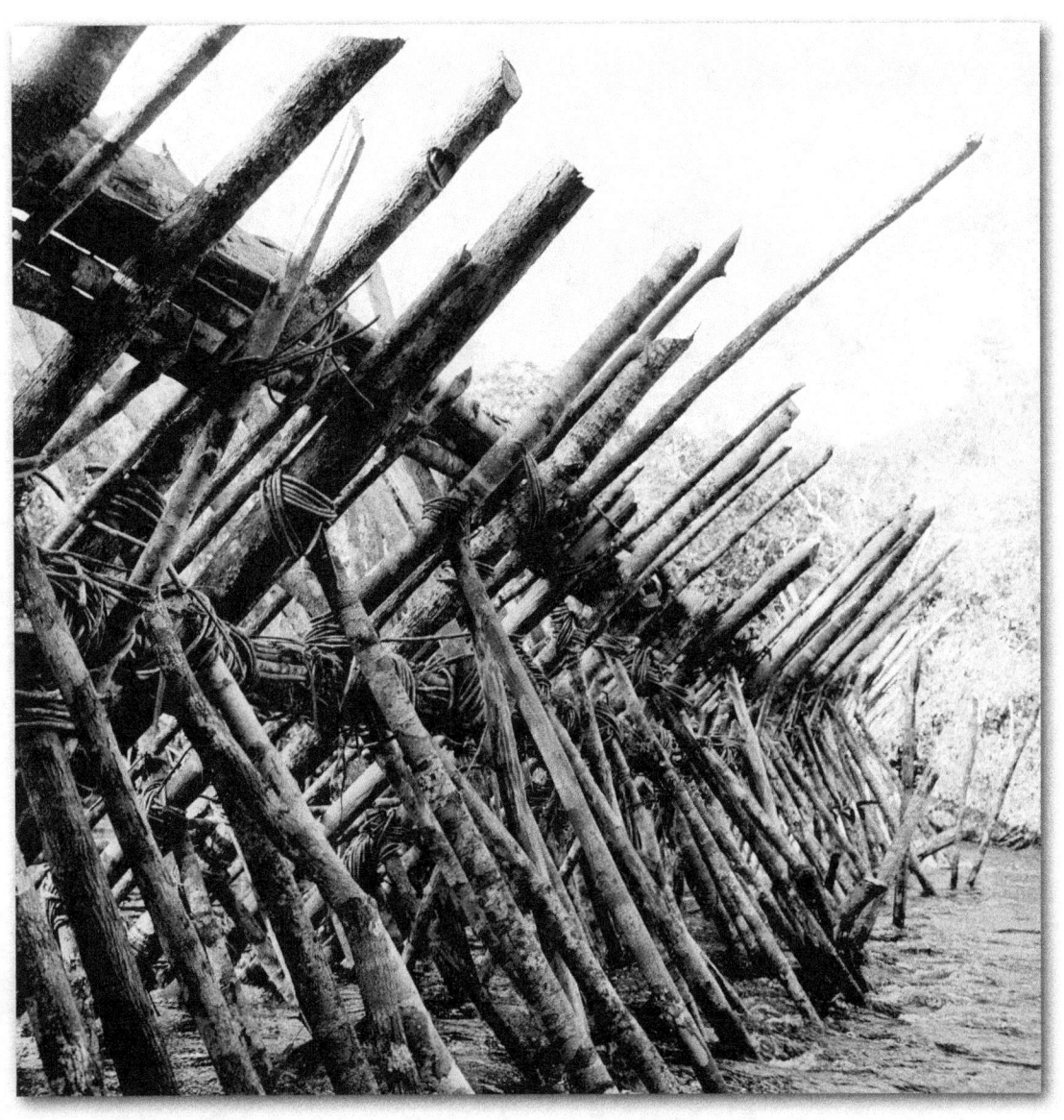

Tradicional River Damm fishing structure

2008

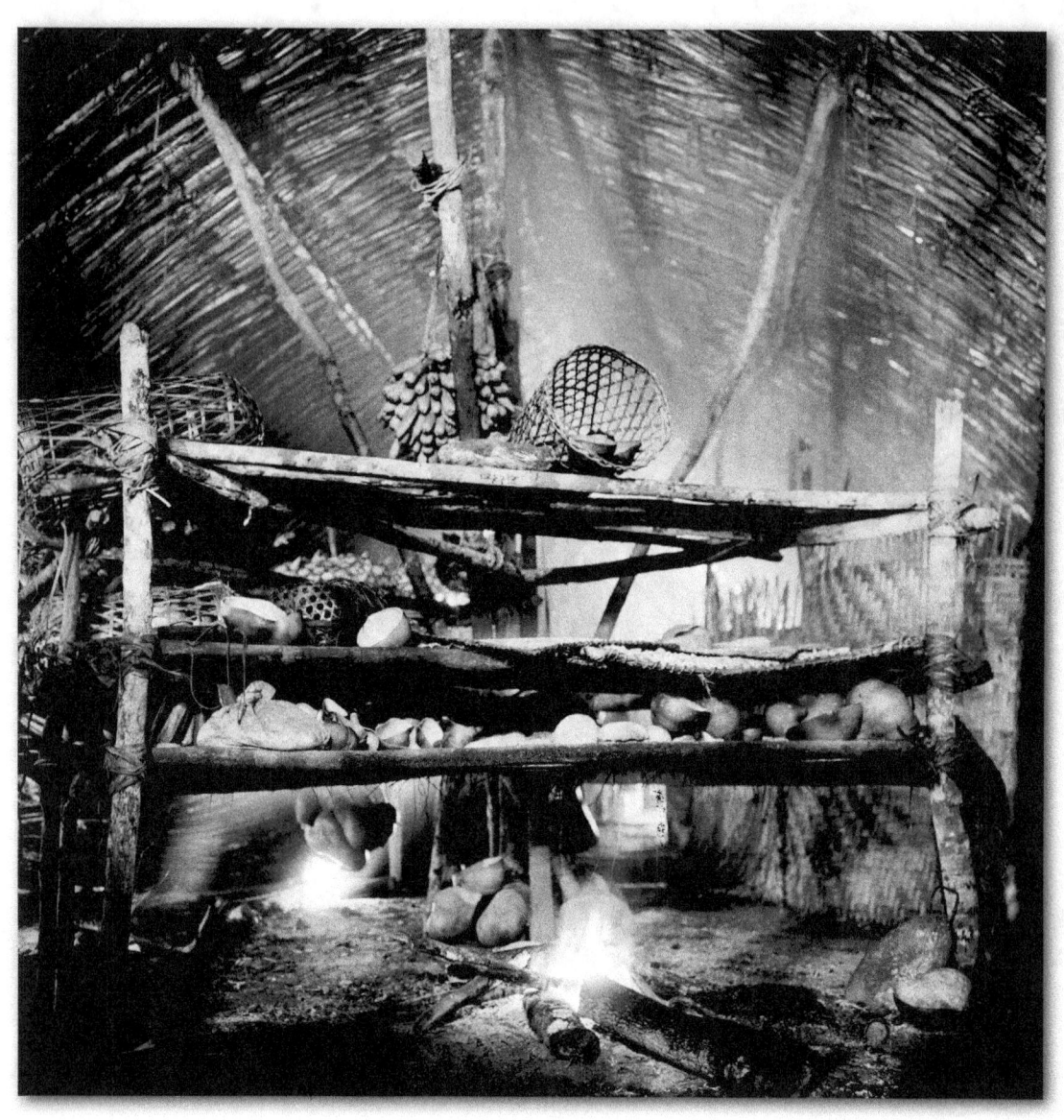

Enawenê-Nawê coocking rack

2008

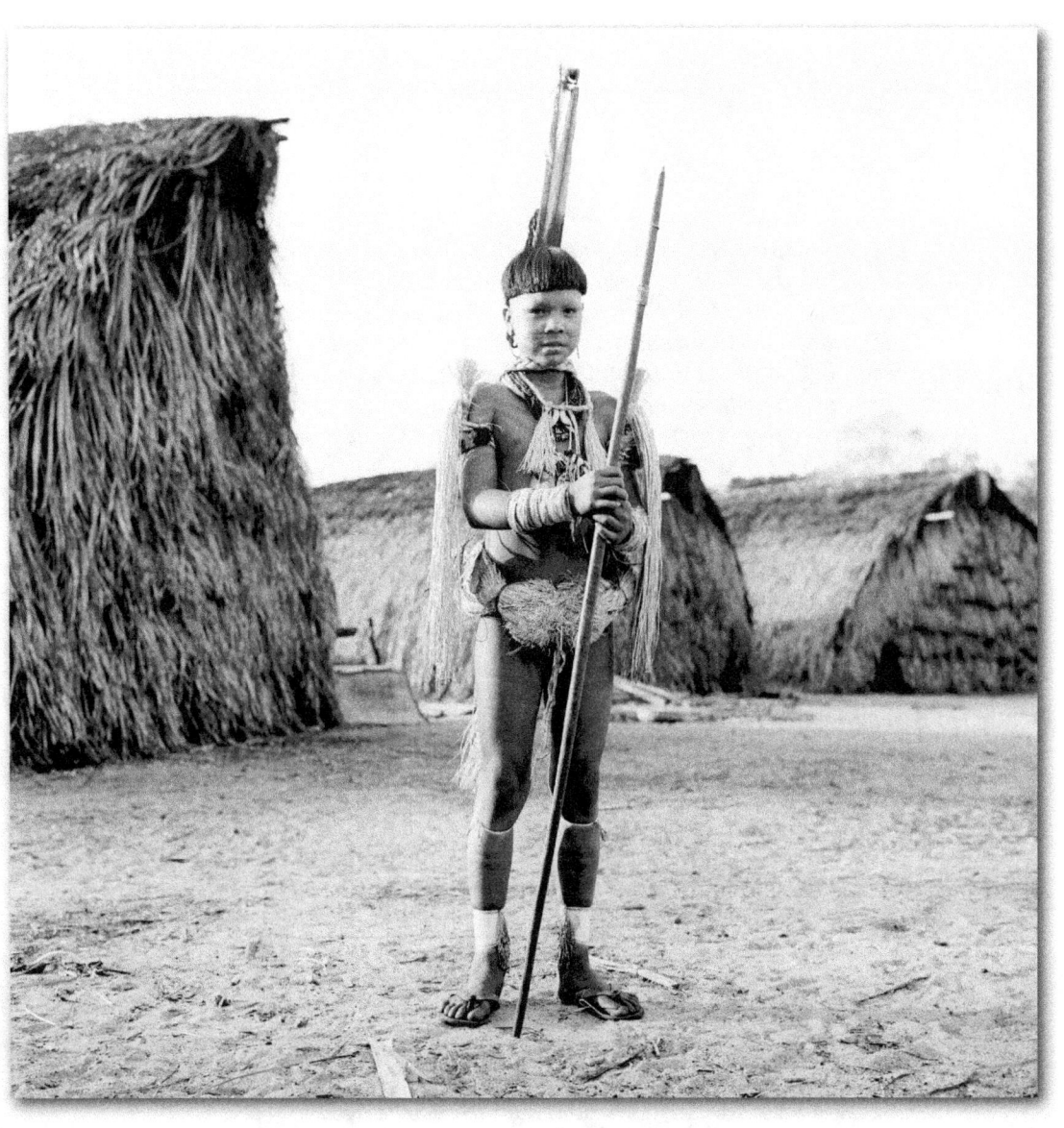

Portrait at the Yãkwa ritual

2008

Kayapó

Speakers of a Jê language, the Mebêngôkre, which mean "people from the water hole" in their native language, are called Kayapó by neighboring groups, meaning "those who look like monkeys". They used to live in a territory known as Caiapônia, which spread from the region just south of Goiás state to the northern portion of old São Paulo province, according to Aires de Casal. Today they live in the states of Pará and Matogrosso, counting amongst their population some 8000 people divided into seven subgroups: Gorotire, Kuben-Krân-Krên, Kôkraimôrô, Kararaô, Mekrãgnoti, Metyktire and Xikrin.

Kôkô, or Kwot-Kwot*, is a ceremony during which some Mebêngôkre are given special names. Those who are given these names have, from that moment on, the permanent right to bear the prefix kôkô before their names, e. g. Kôkôjam. They are also forbidden to eat food derived from animals that participated at the event, as well as being obligated to attend to other celebrations, because they are also Kôkô. During these celebrations, they make masks with different kinds of straw and techniques representing the pàt (anteater), the kubut (a capuchin monkey), the kukôire (a howler monkey) and the kôkô (a kind of fish).

The ritual also has implications for the complex political articulations among many communities and subgroups, as well as the specific knowledge and skills for the making of the elaborate masks. Between February and April 2008, I had the opportunity to photograph these experts at different phases of the preparation of masks and at the ritual celebration in Kayapó Indigenous Territory, South of Pará state.

The names were written according to the orientation of the natives themselves

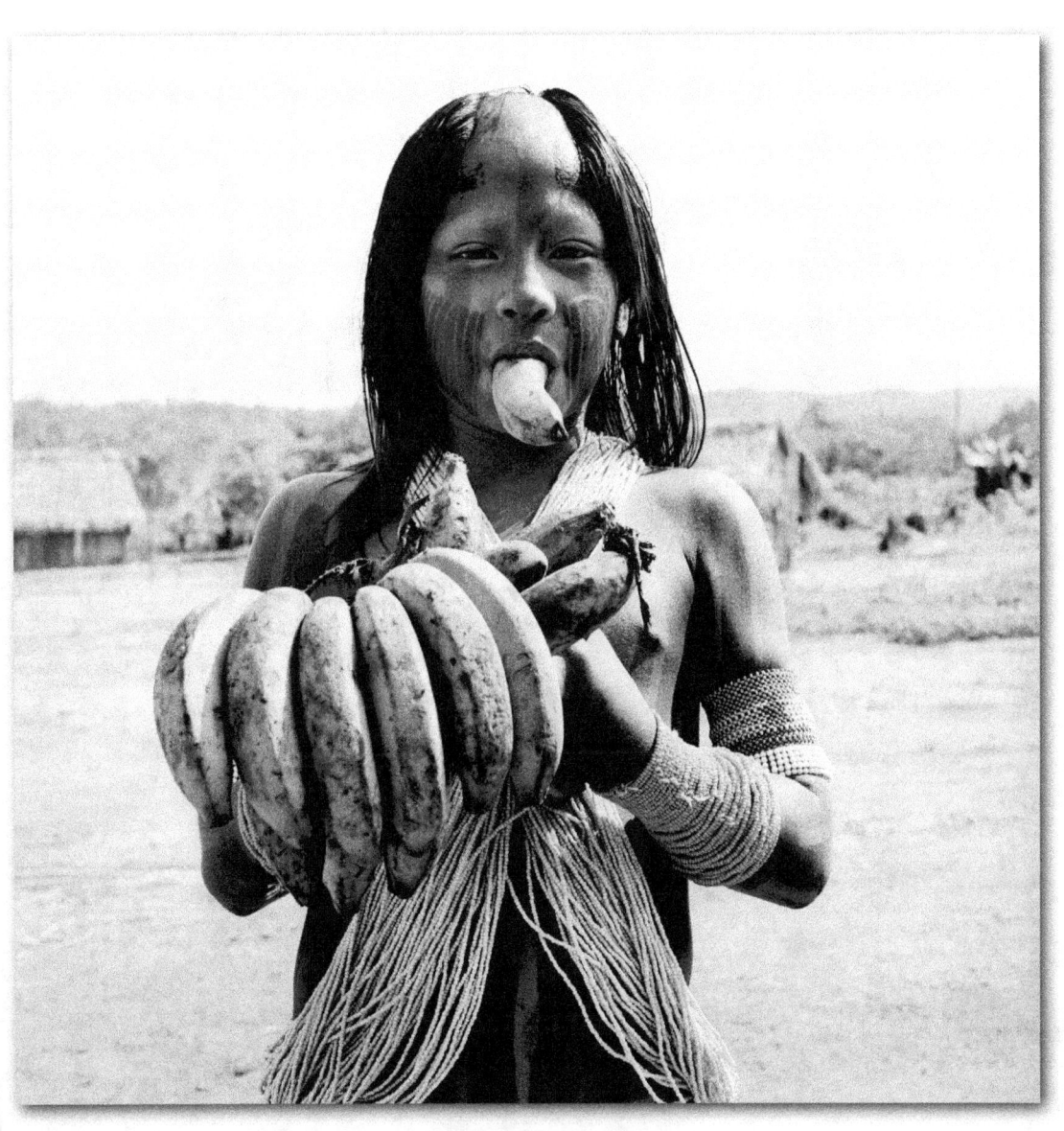

Kayapó Mebengokrê / Kriny community
southern Pará, circa Redenção 2007

79

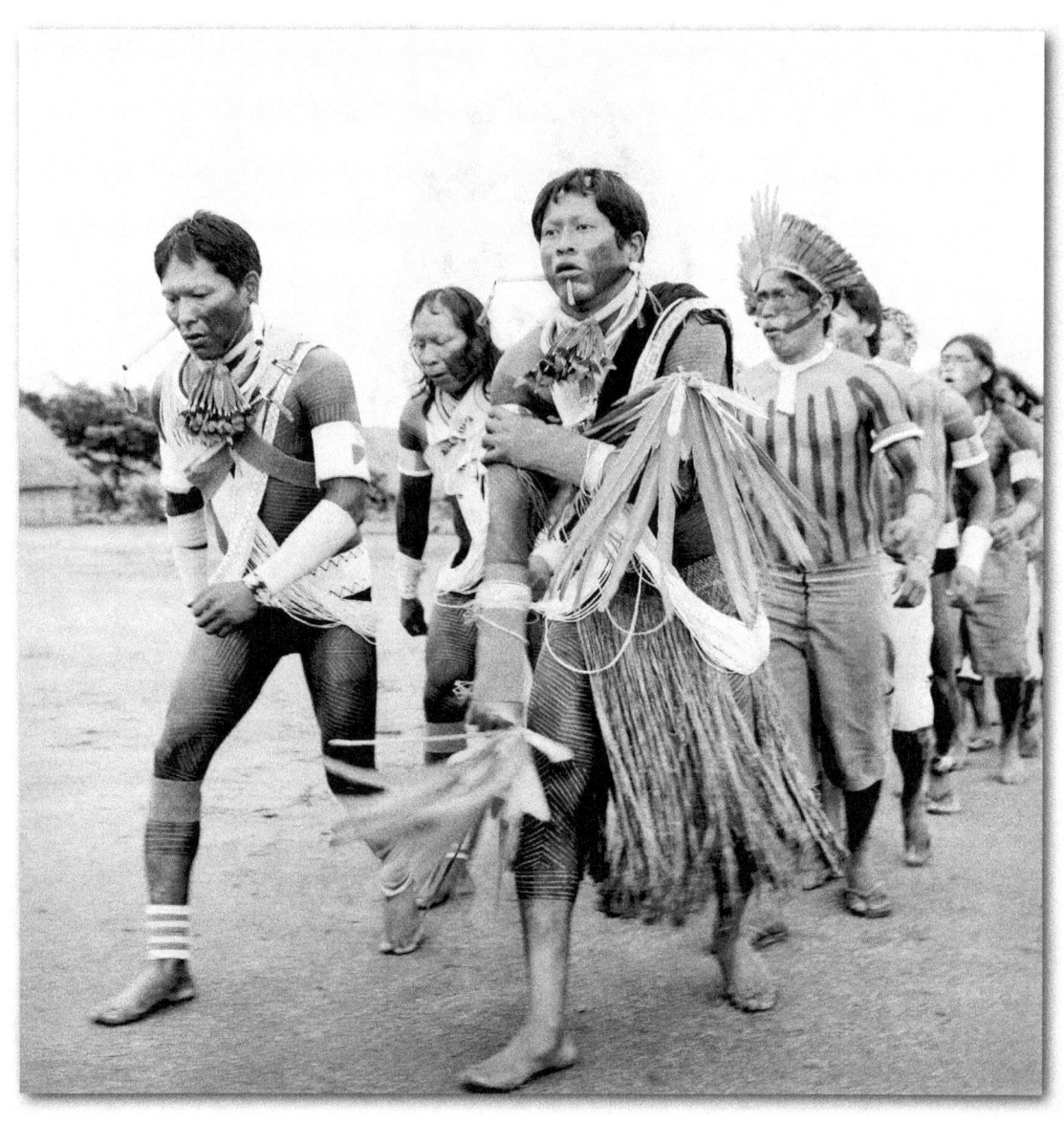

Male dance / Memy Toro

2007

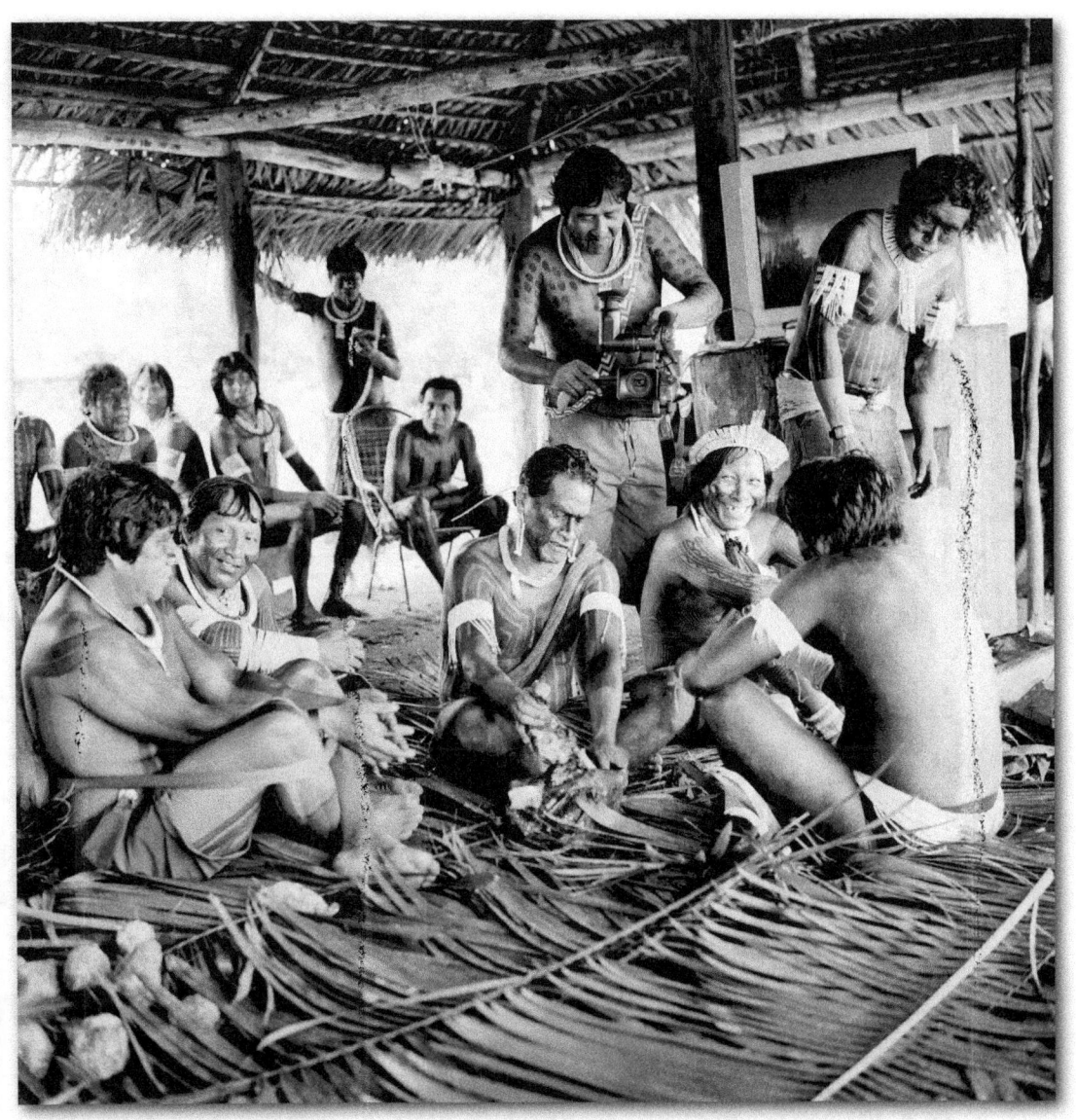

Men 's lunch (tortoise) at the warrior's house (Ngã)

2007

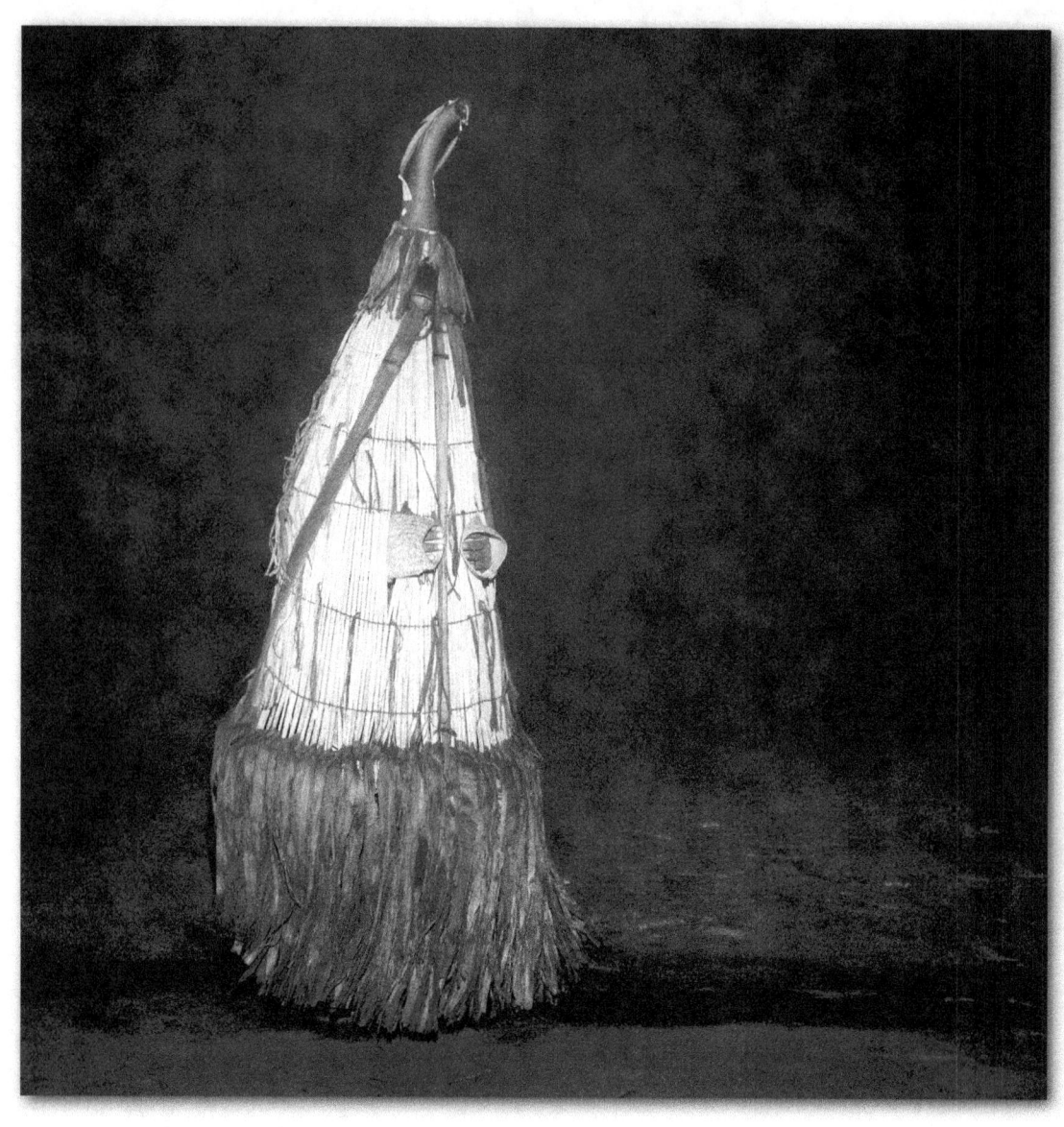

Pàt Mask (Anteater) / Late night appearance

2007

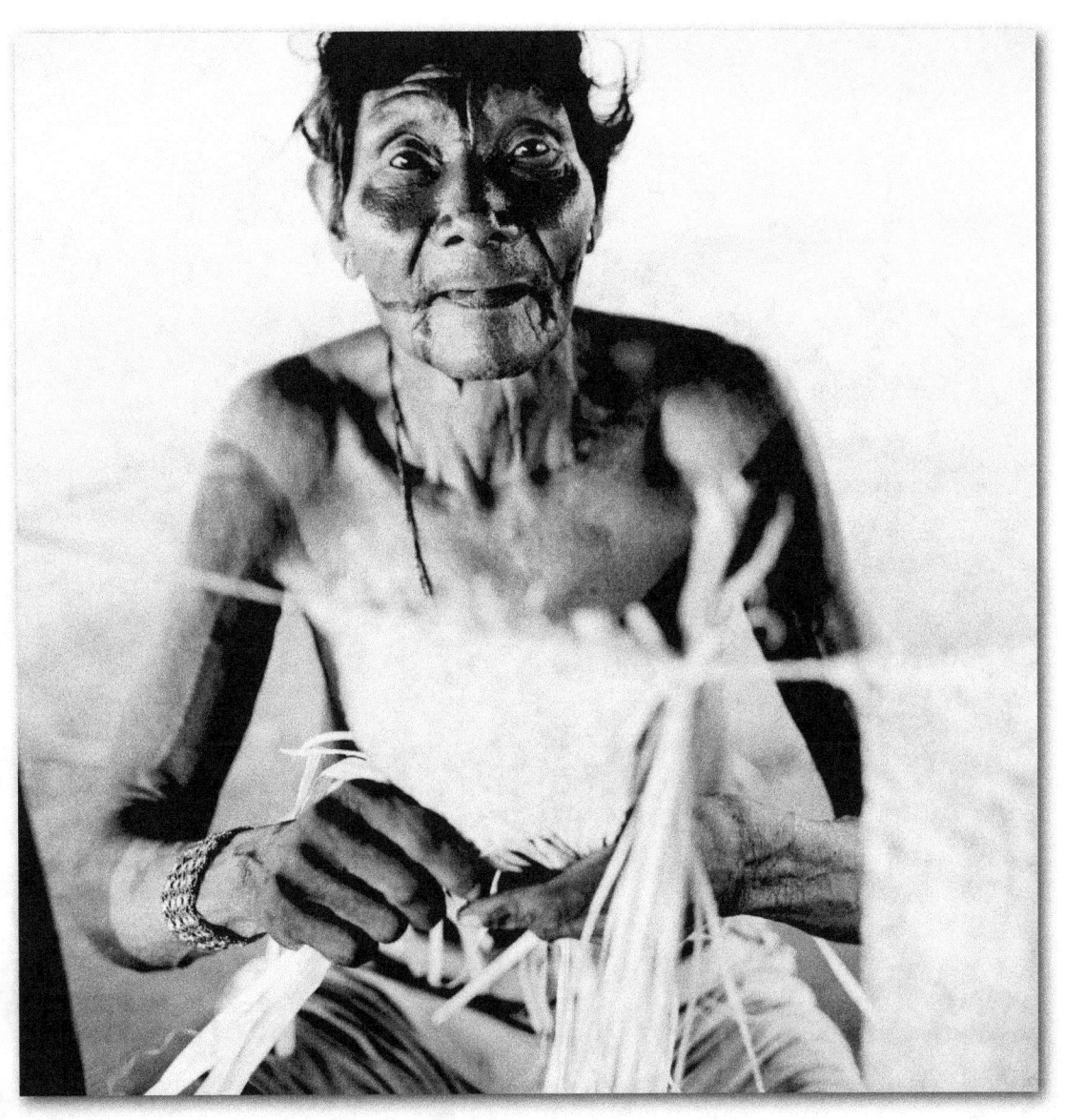

Mask expert maker (Me ayry djwynh)

2007

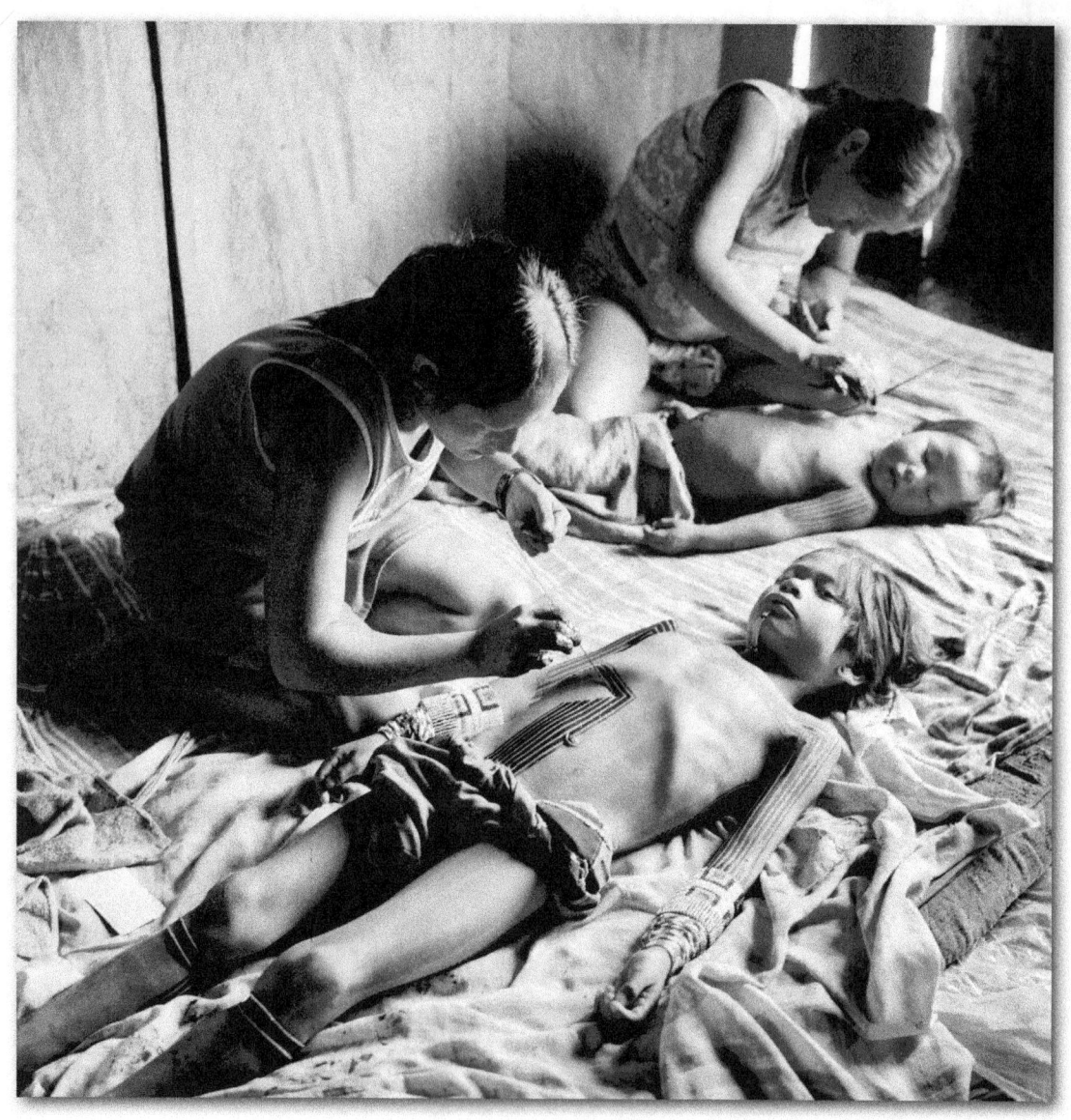

Preparing the children for the Kowt-Kwot celebration (Me prire ôk)

2007

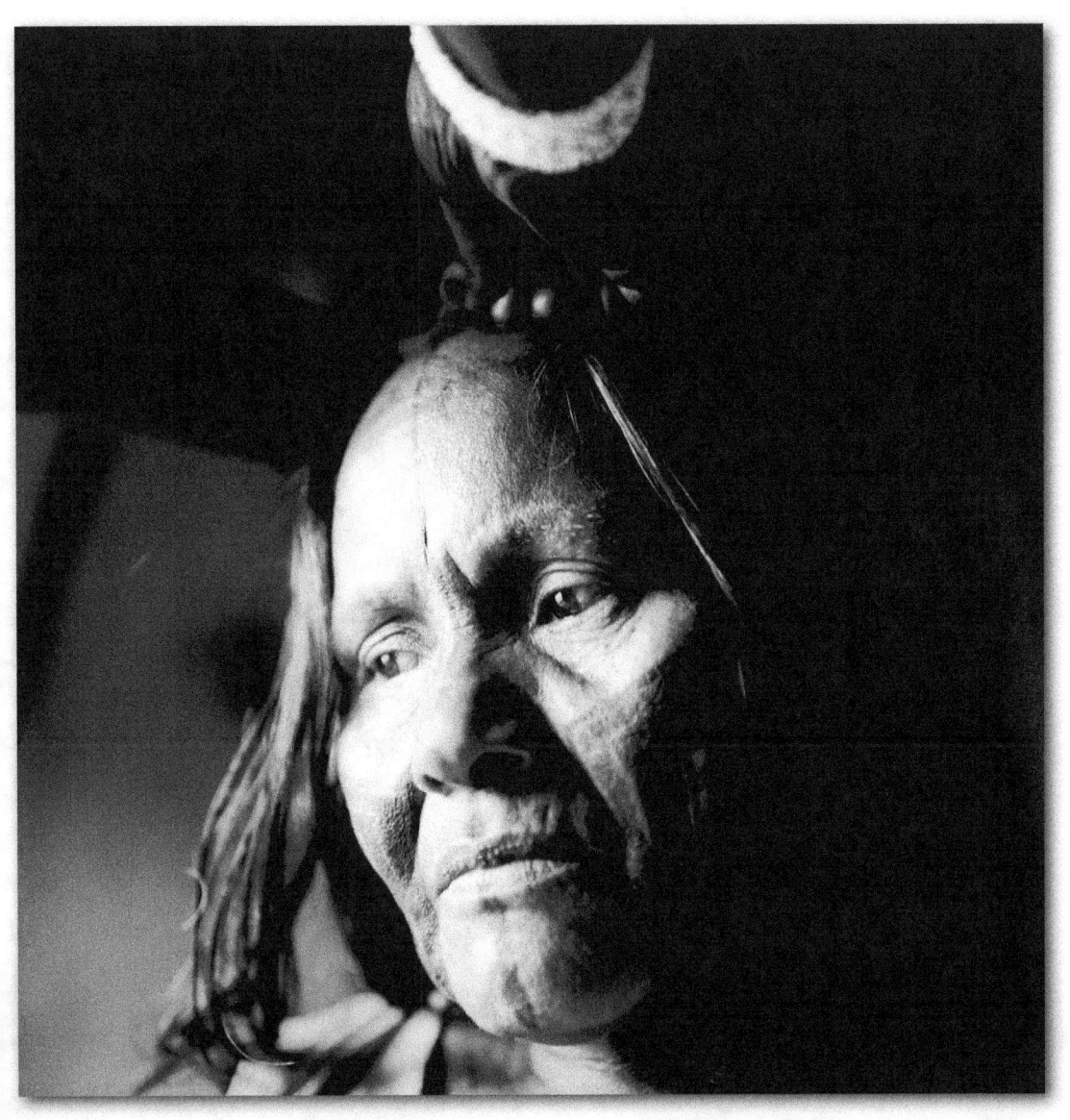

Tradicional hair cut (Me ijokàra)

2007

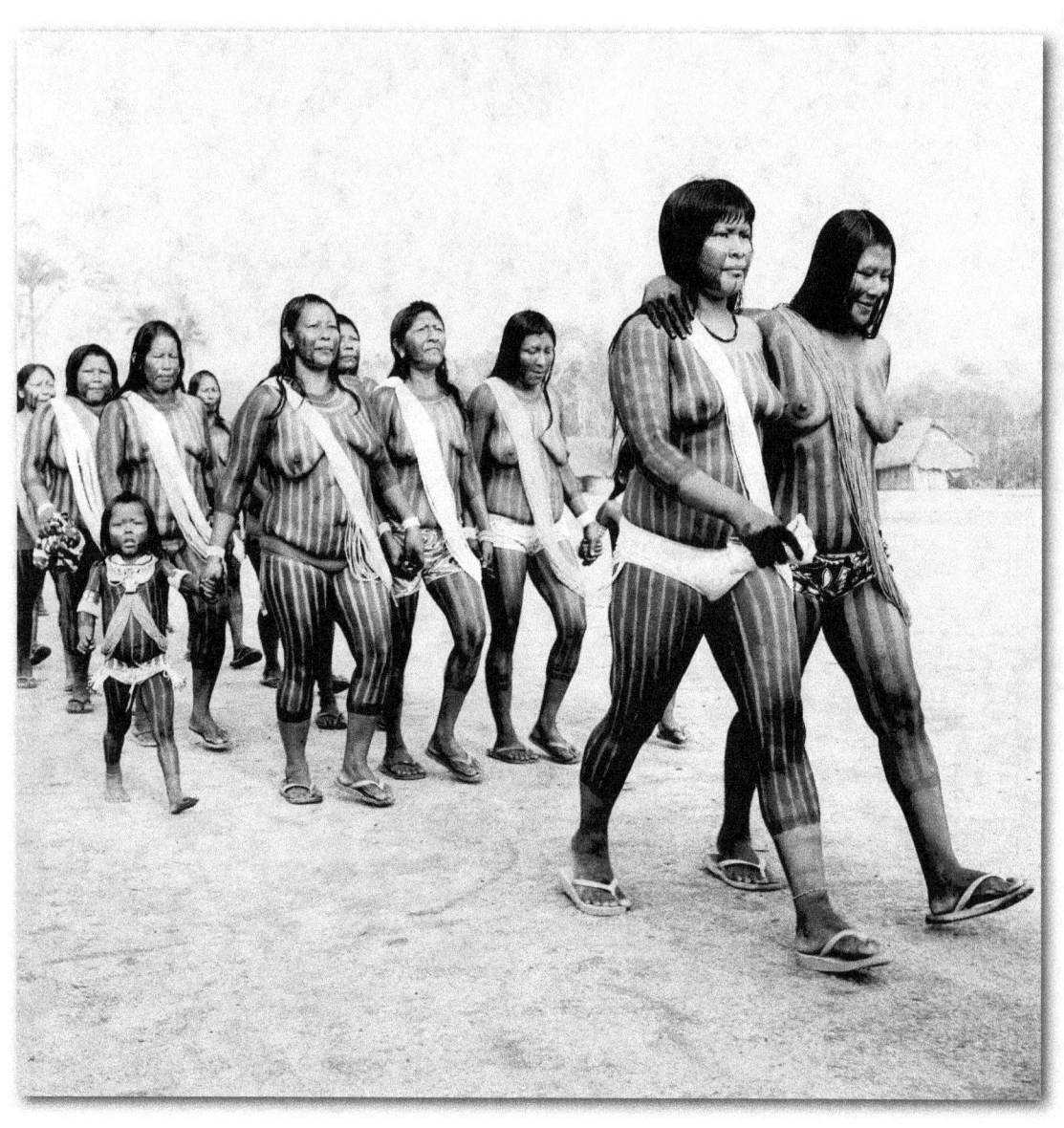

Dance from the cassava celebration (Kwyrkangô ã me toro)

2007

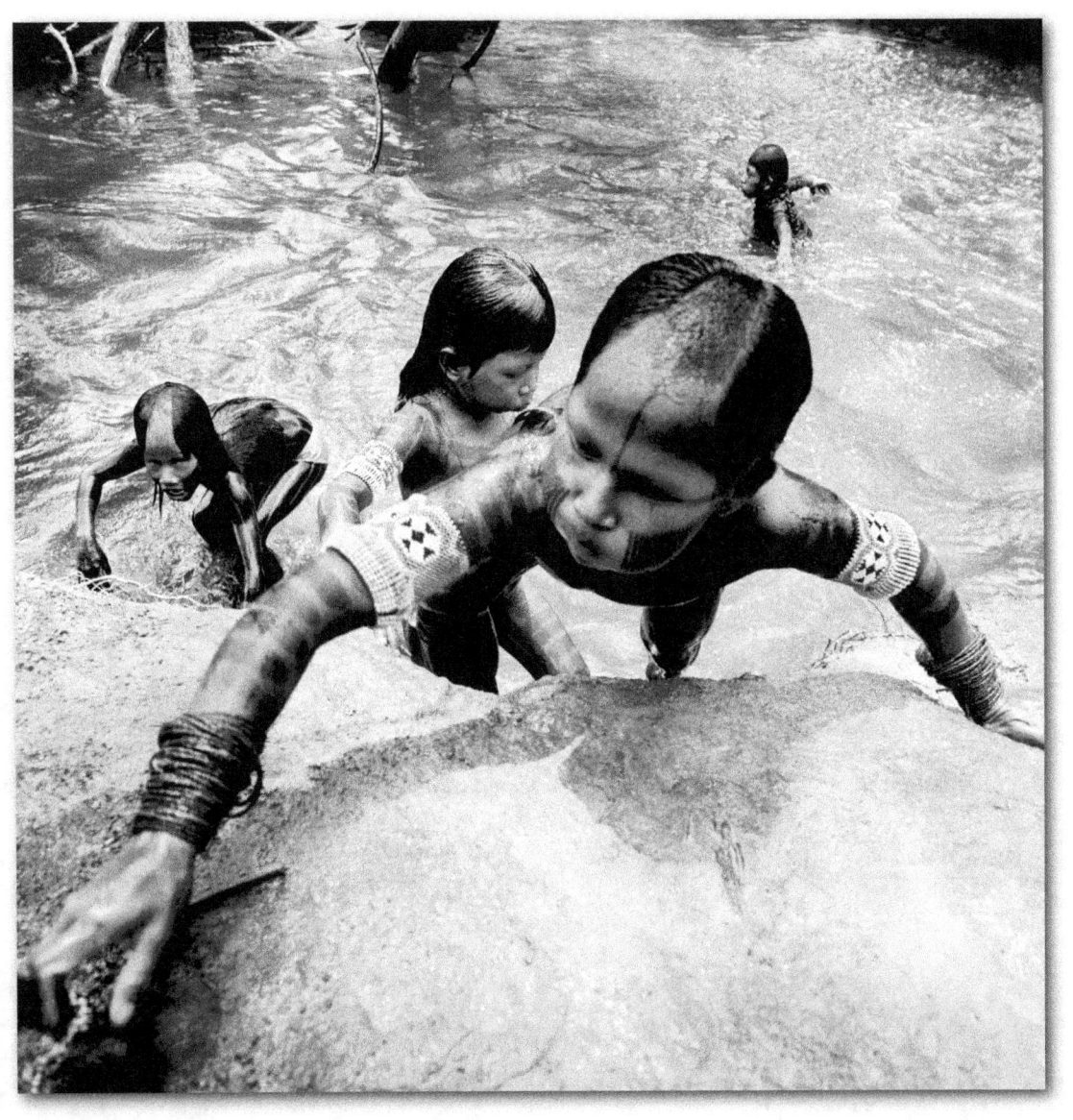

Bath at Fresco River (Ngôja kriti)

2007

Xavante

The Xavantes, self-styled A'uwe ("people), are an ethnic group who are speakers of a Jê language, whose contact with non-indigenous society dates back to the mid 18th century. Back then, the Xavantes lived in the northern and central portions of what is now Goiás state. They moved, however, towards the southwest in order to avoid contact with the colonizers. Contact was established again in the 1930s, but they were "pacified" only by the end of the 1940s. Today, squeezed amongst the agricultural frontiers, the 18000 Xavantes live in the state of Mato Grosso.

I visited the village of São Marcos, near Barra do Garças, Mato Grosso, in September 2007. By this time of the year, the weather is marked by hot days with dry air and blue skies. The sunlight is penetrating, hurting the eyes, while the nights are cold. Located in the Cerrado, the land has sandy soil, and is dotted with small vegetation.

There I photographed their buriti log race, called uiwede in Xavante language. The two teams that form the organizational structure of the Xavante society take part in the competition, the poriza'õno and the öwawe. Each participant does his utmost effort to carry a log on their shoulders over short circuits, passing the log to another member of the team until they finish the competition in the center of the village. Weighing approximately 80 kilos, the extremely heavy logs are transported over irregular routes that vary between 6 and 8 kilometers.

A women's race also exists, with slightly lighter logs. The race participants are always adults of the same sex. Also, I had the opportunity to photograph a group singing and dancing performance called da-ño're. This dance, which is performed after the race, is also a competition between the teams which structure the Xavante society. This is, however, a singing and dancing competition in which men almost exclusively take part, unlike the race.

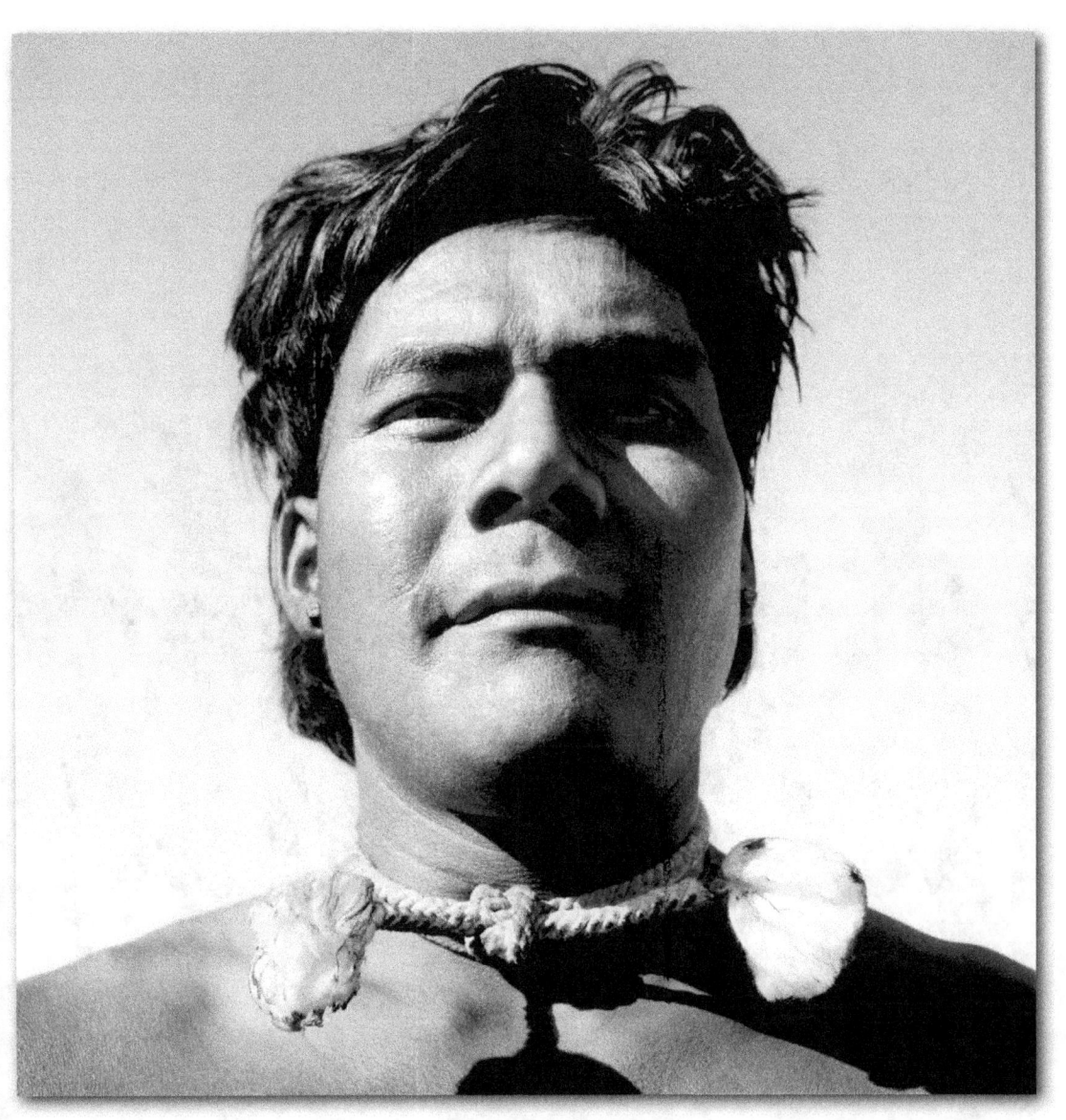

Xavante / Portrait wearing a tradicional cotton tie (Dañorebzu'a)

Mato Grosso 2007

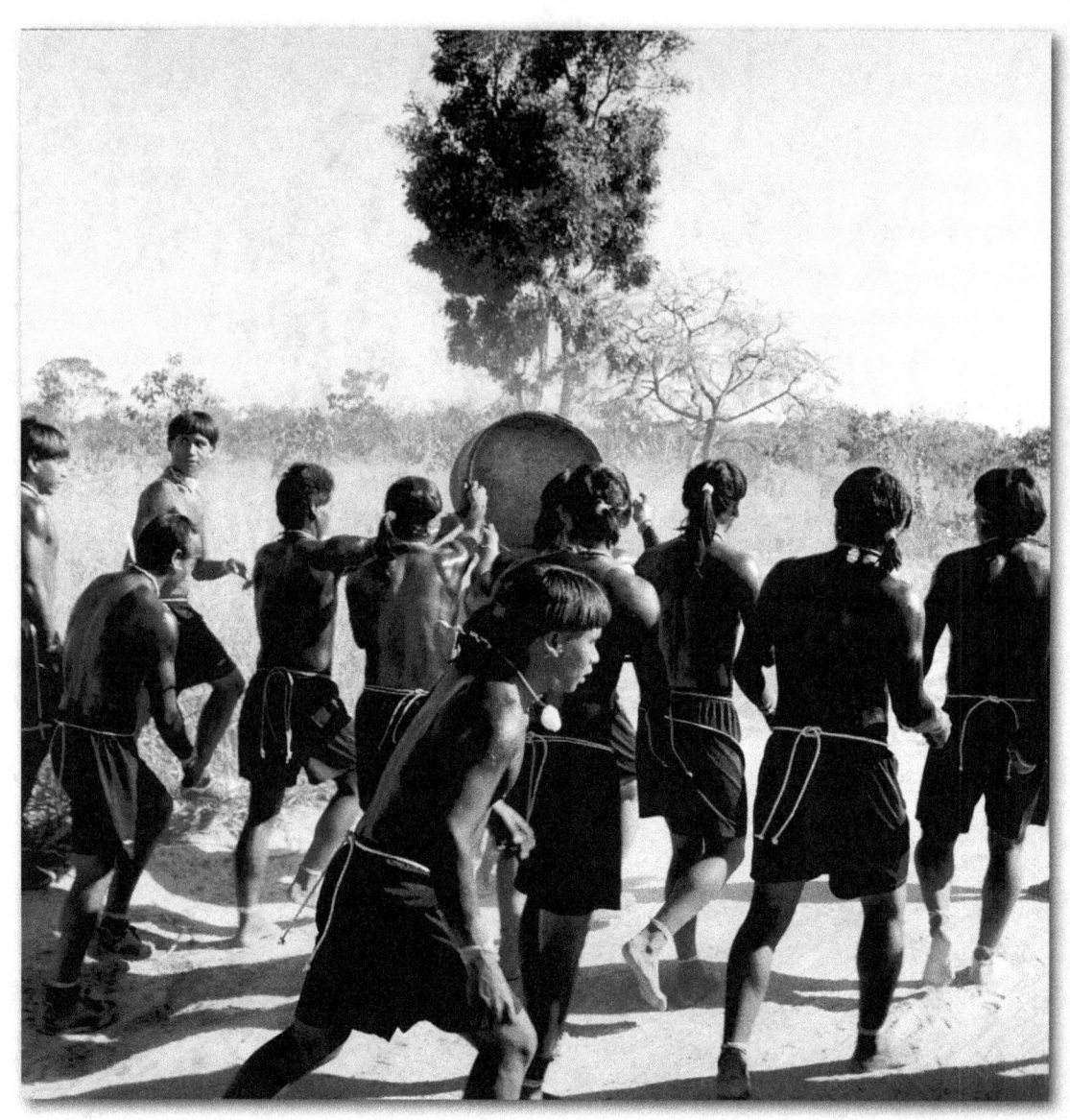

Buriti log race (Uiwêde)

2007

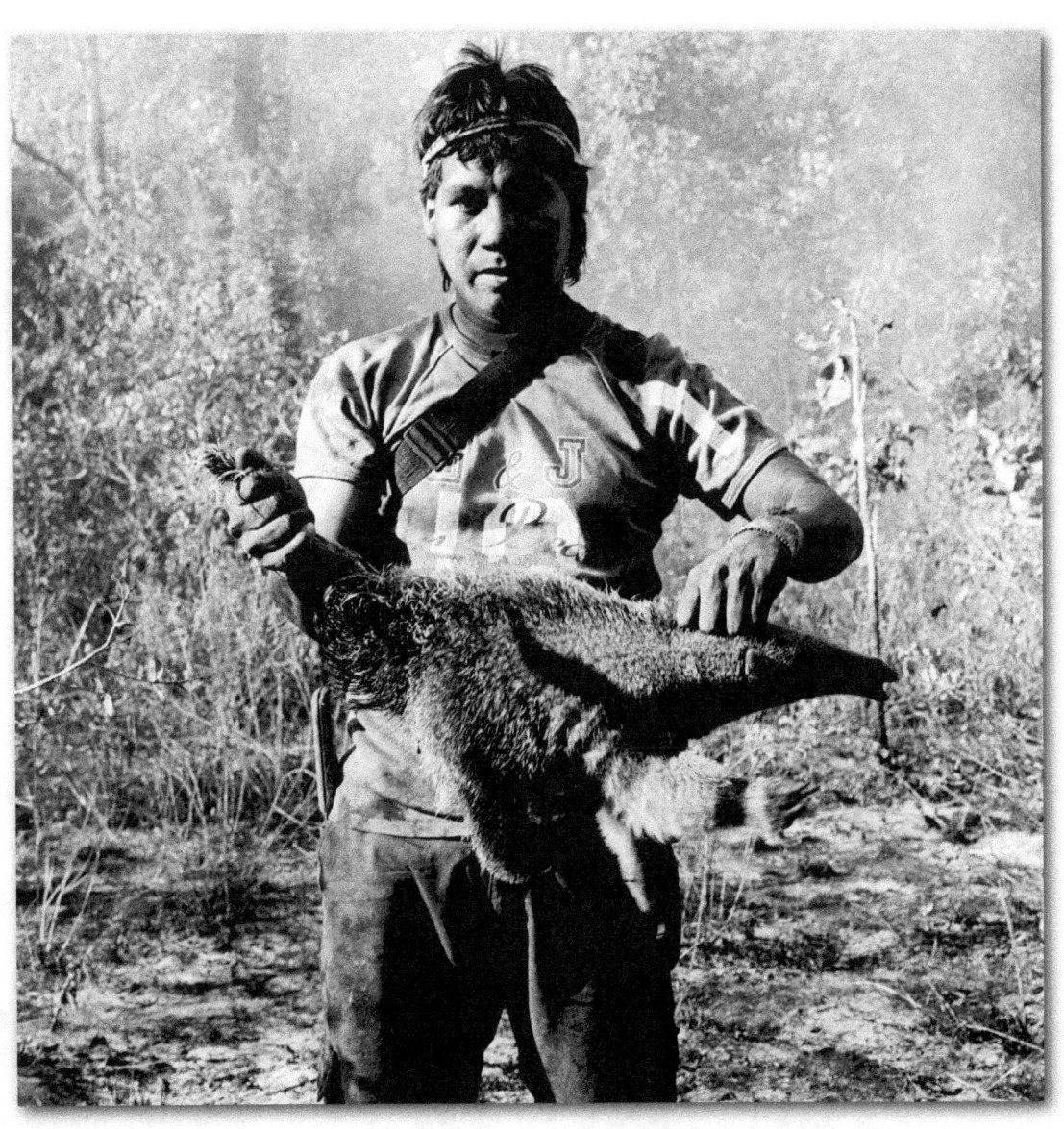

Hunt aftermath/ Small anteater (Myrmecophaga tridactyla)

2007

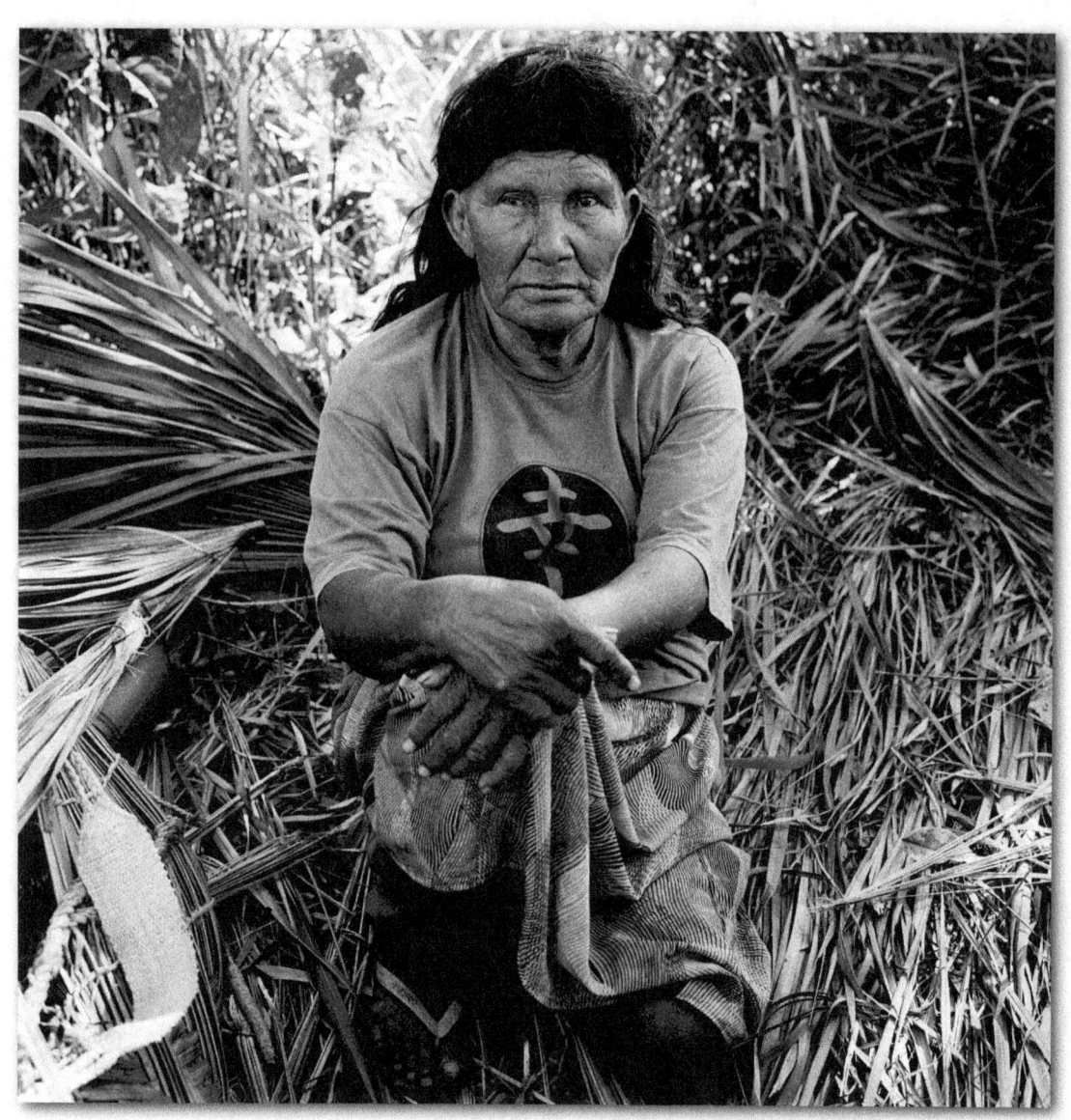

Harvest of the Titica vine (Heteropsis flexuosa)

2007

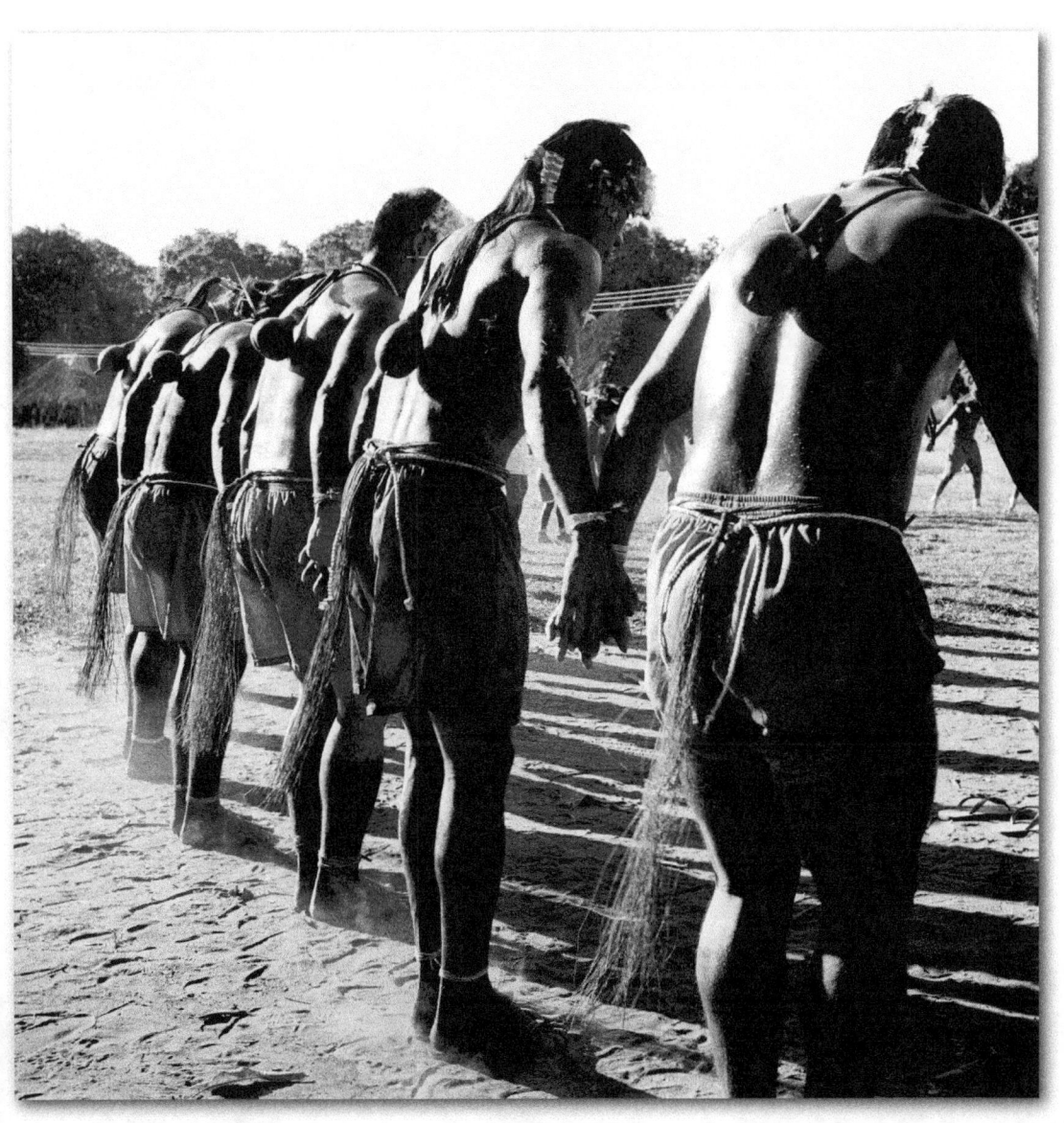

Colective male ceremony (Da-ño're)

2007

Land & identity

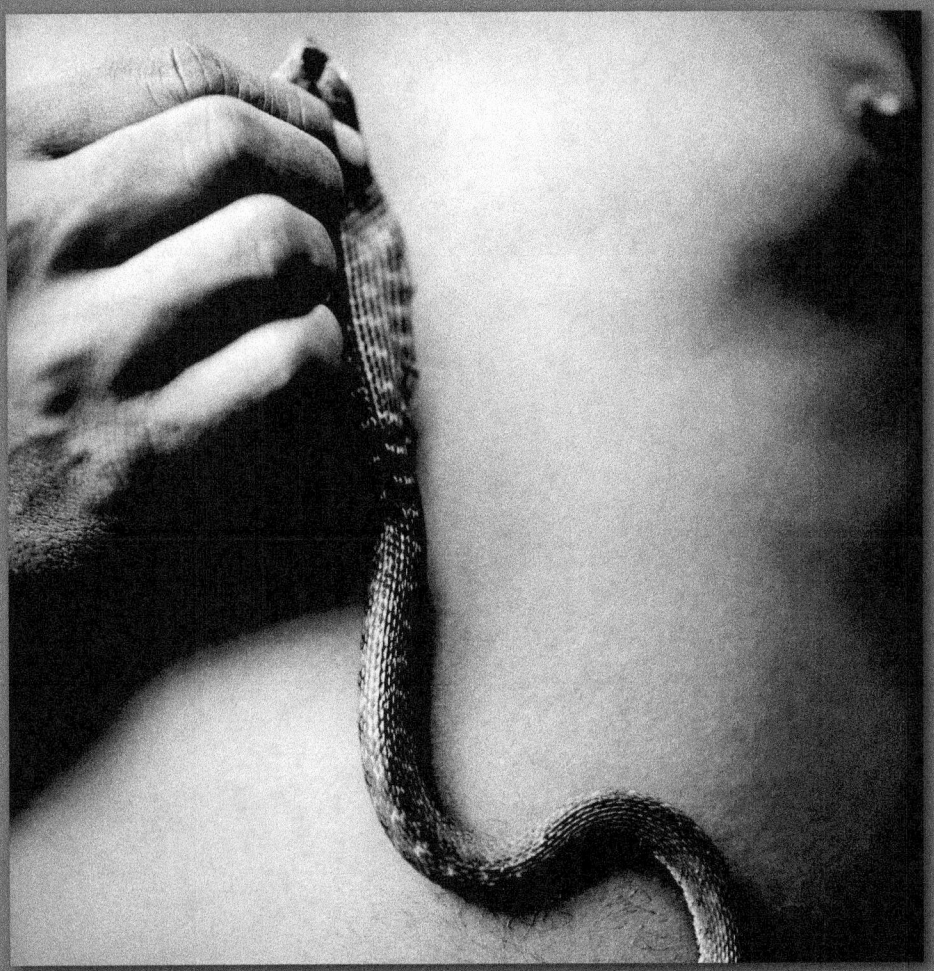

Young anaconda (Eunectes murinus) devoring a small fish

Uruapiara River

Composition of ten images in panoramic sequence of igapó (flooded forest) in a 360-degree angle, taken during rainy season, also called winter by locals. The river levels increase more than 10 meters, flooding huge forest areas.

Photographs taken during the rainy season, so-called local winter, on the flooded Ipixuna river. When it meets the Volta Grande river, the two form the Uruapiara river, a Madeira river tributary.

Not very far from this spot, there was once an old Indian Protection Service office. The agency was a precursor of National Indian Foundation (FUNAI), established by Curt Unkel "Nimuendajú" for the Kagwahiva "pacification" in the 1940s.

Romildo da Silva Neves (*1993 †2008), Parintintin Indigenous Land. Photographs taken in March 2005 on a fishing trip near Canavial village.

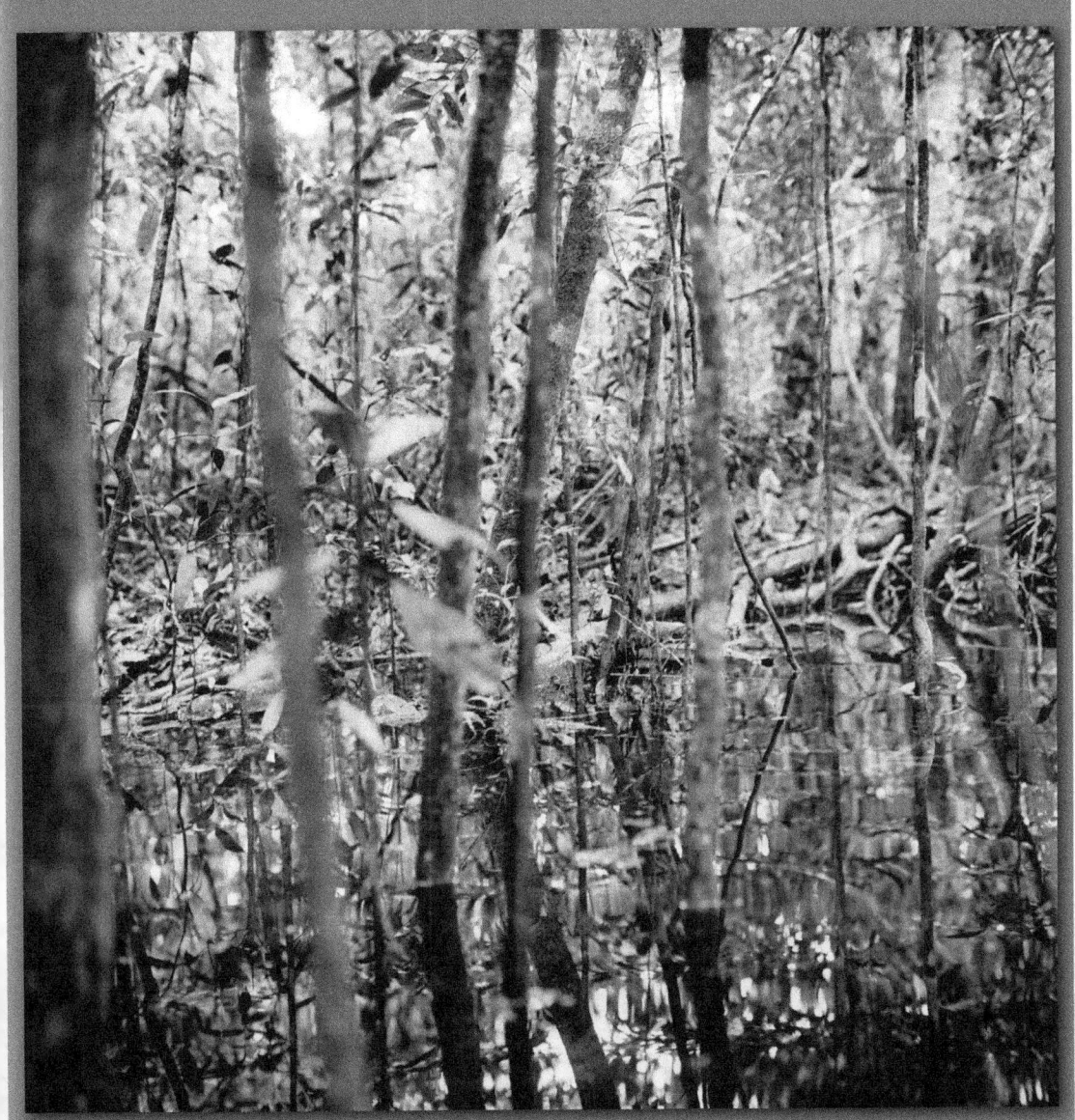

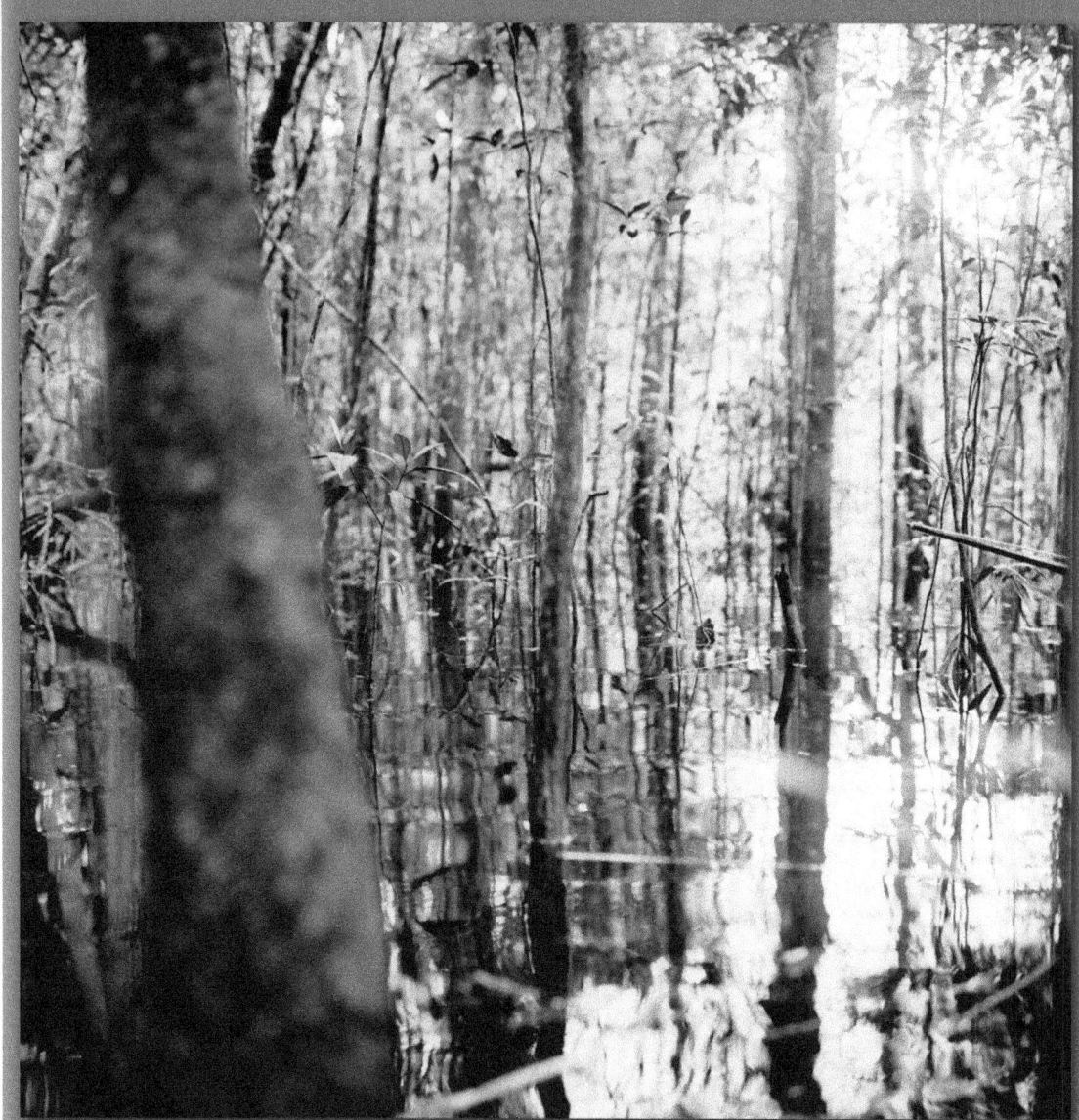

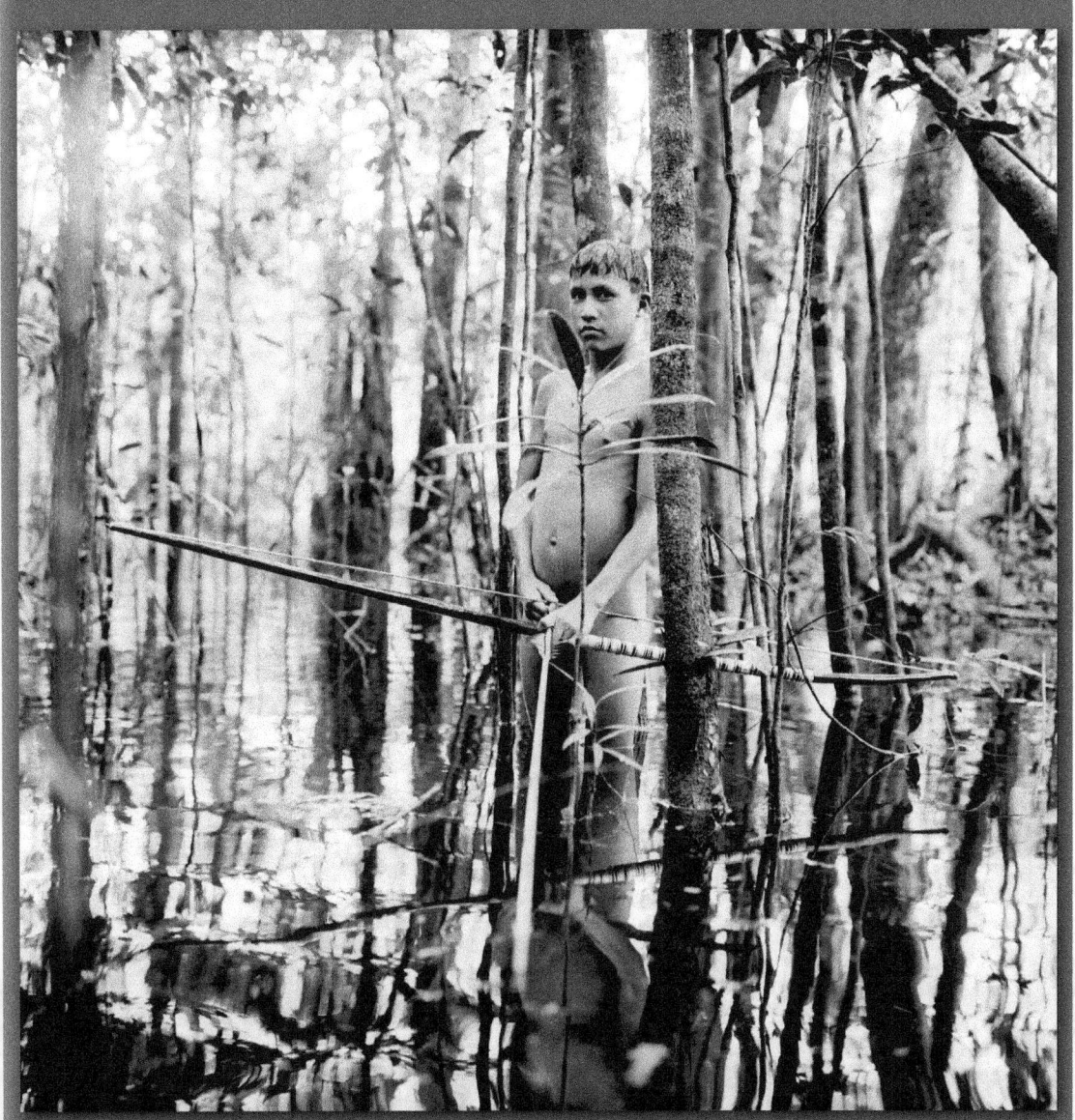

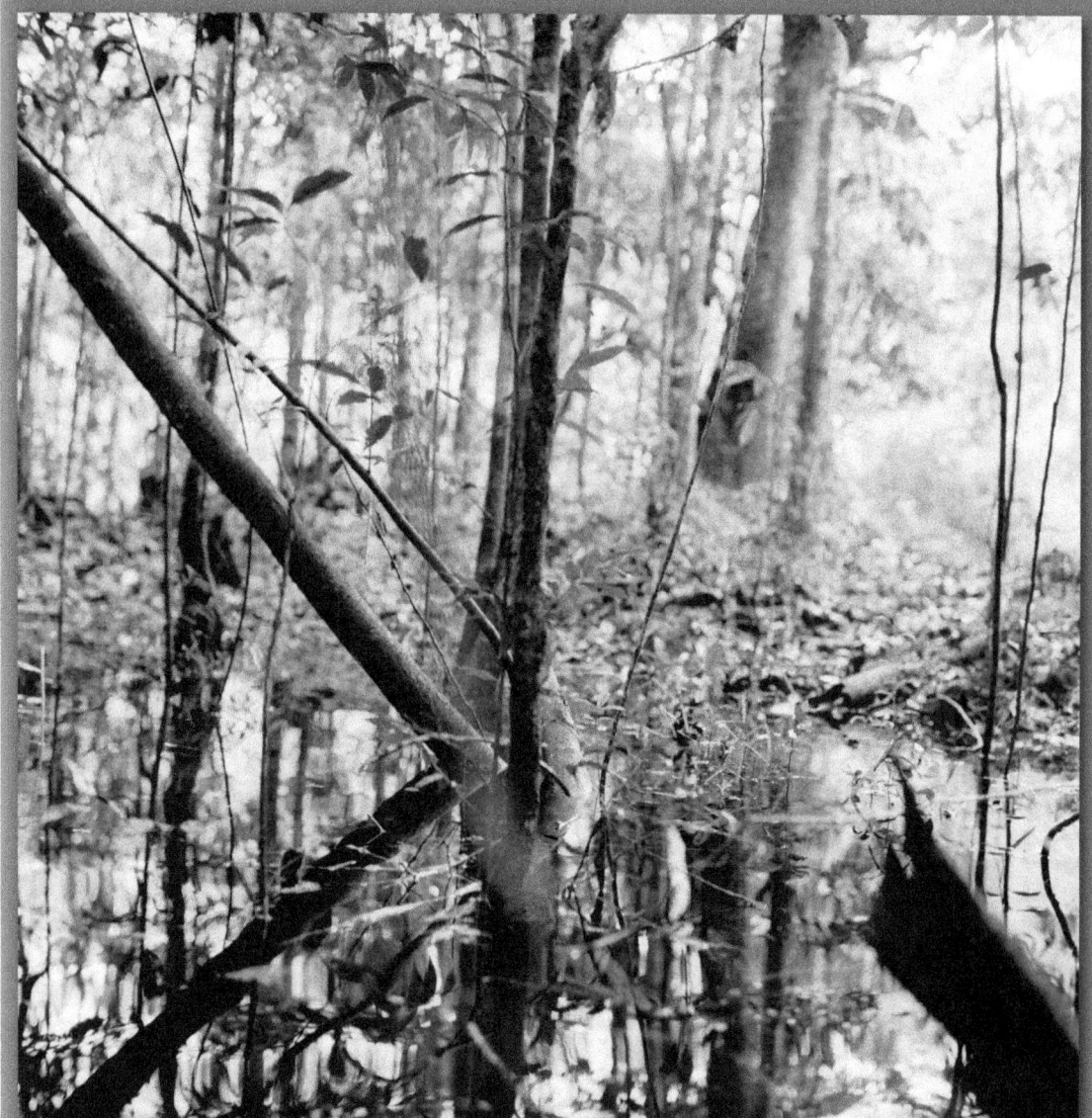

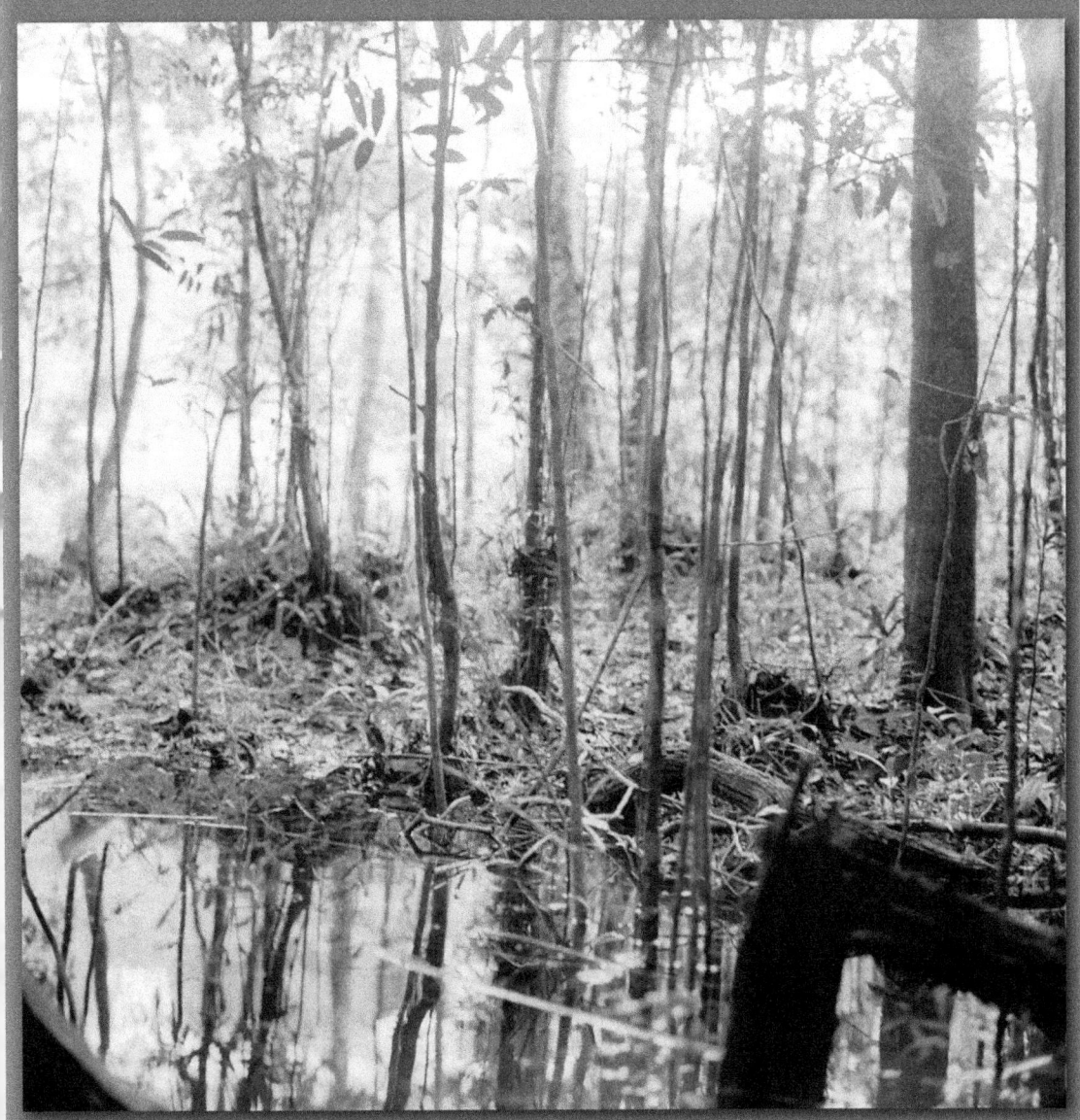

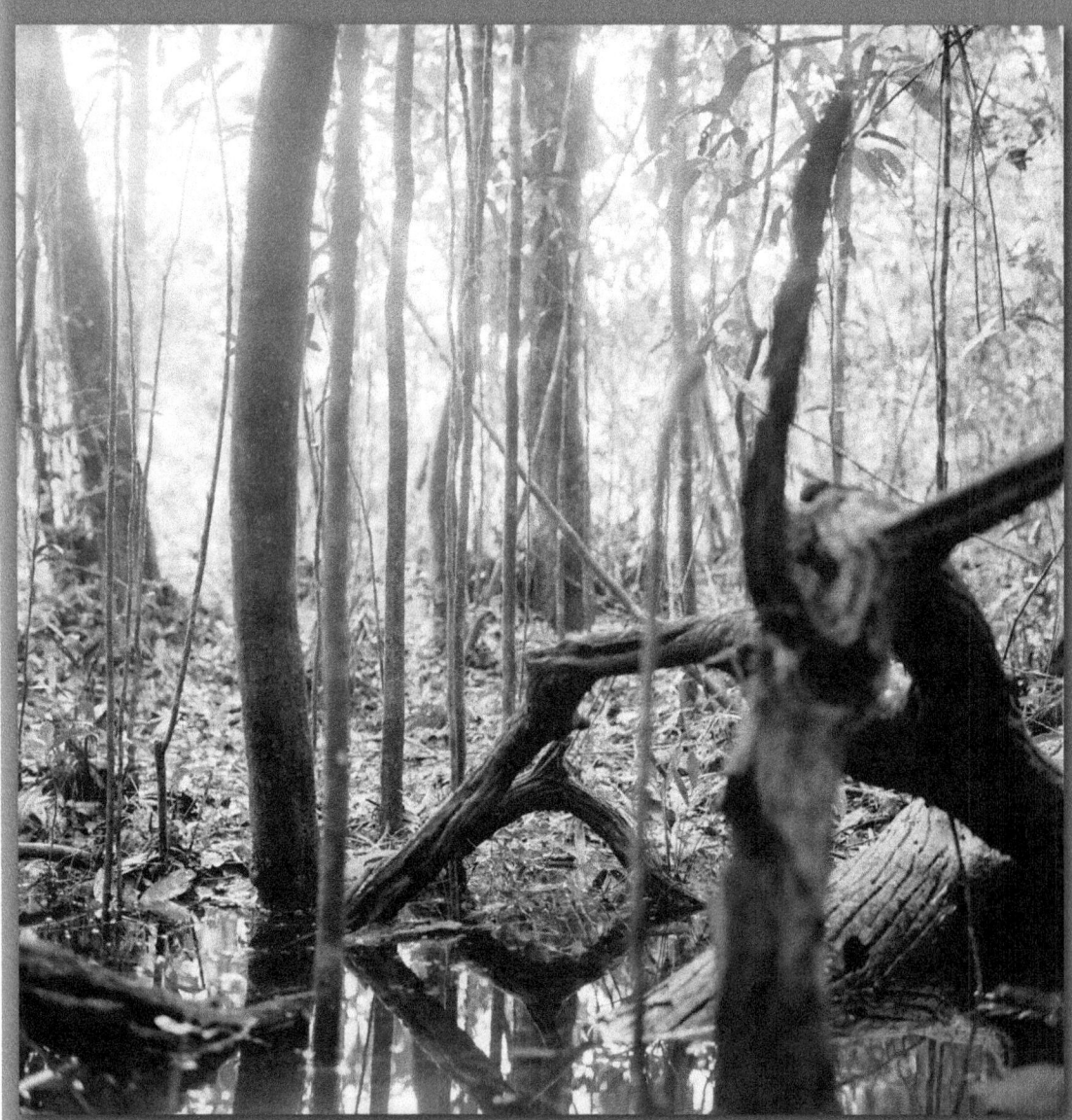

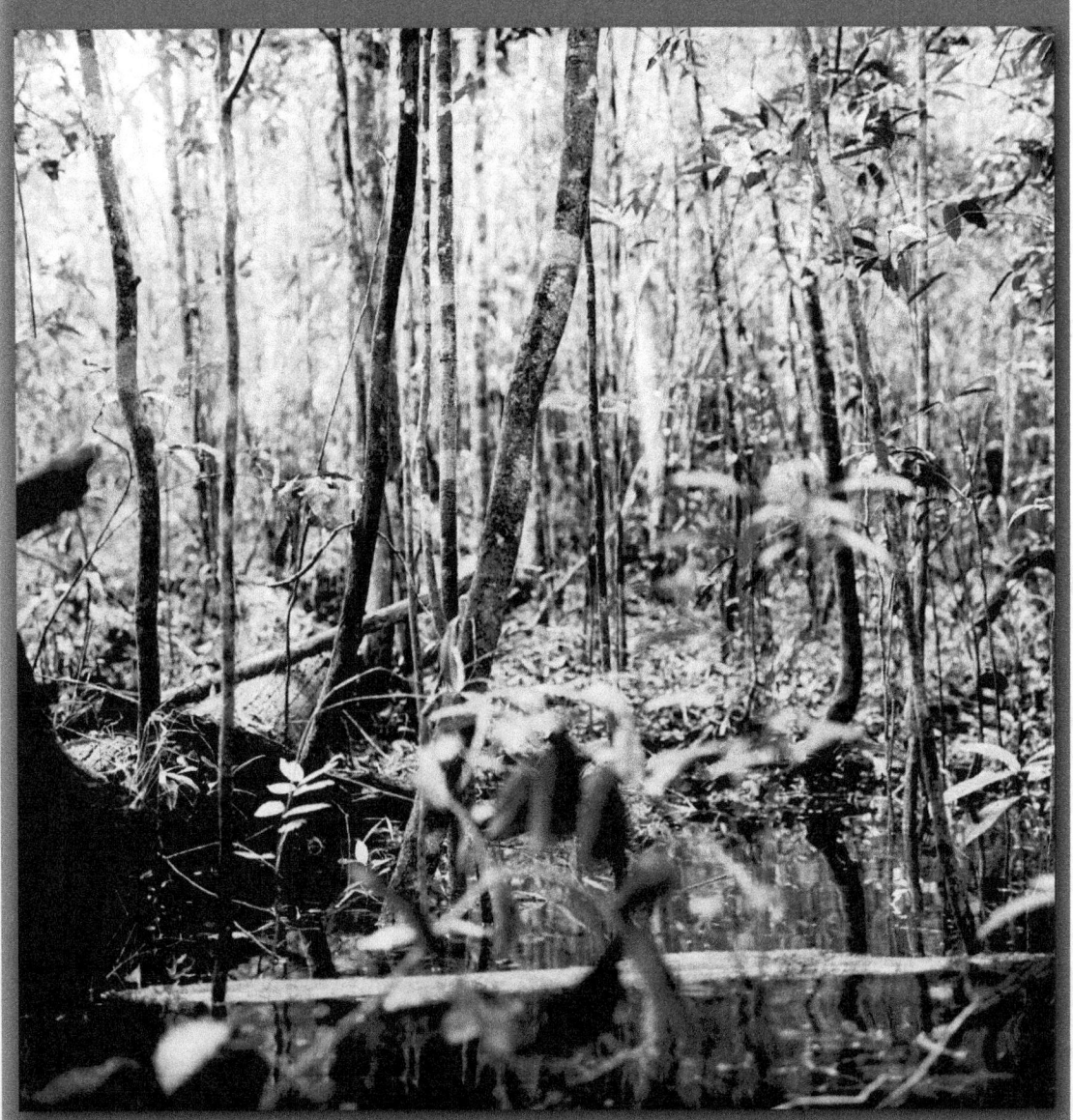

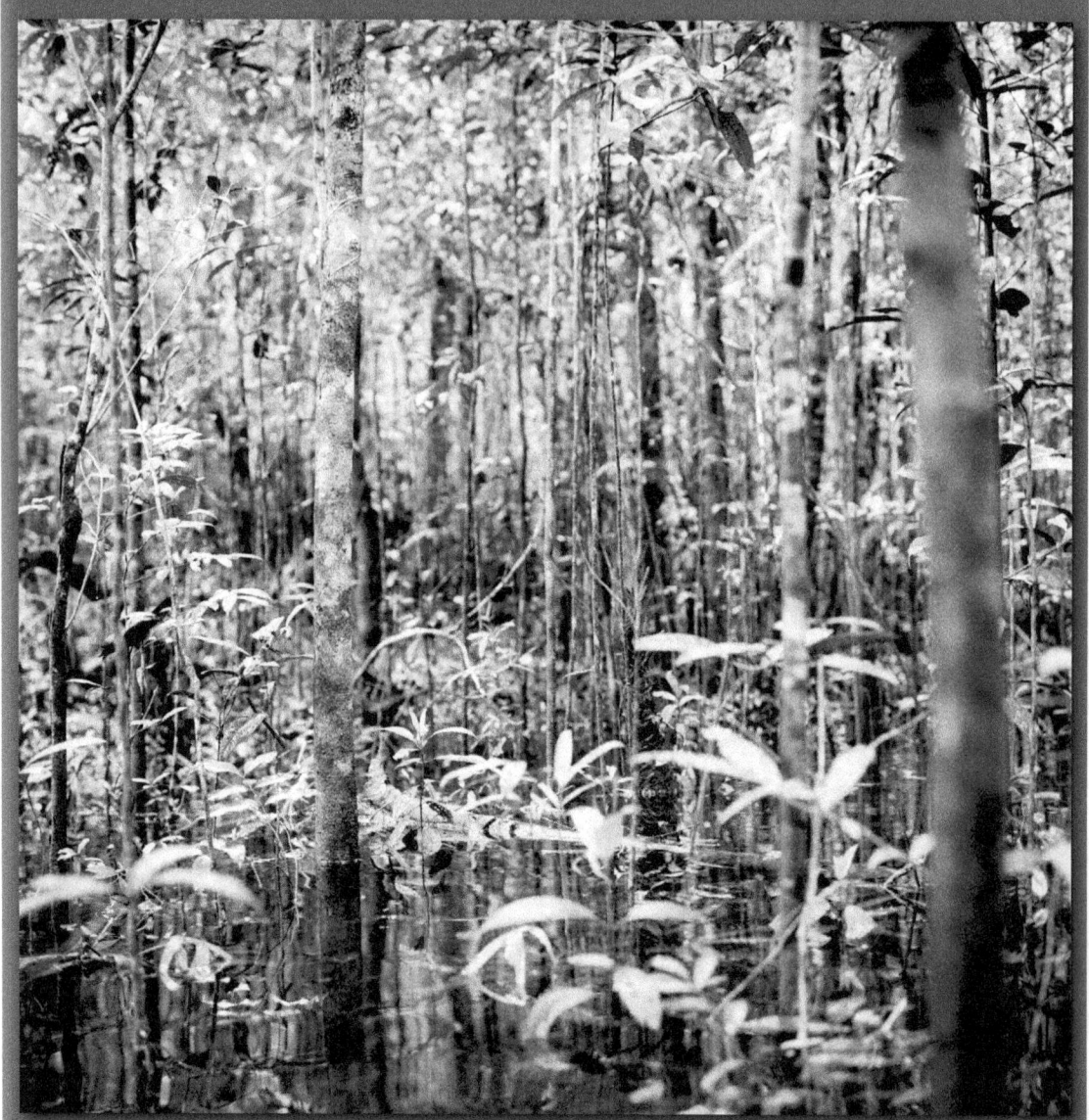

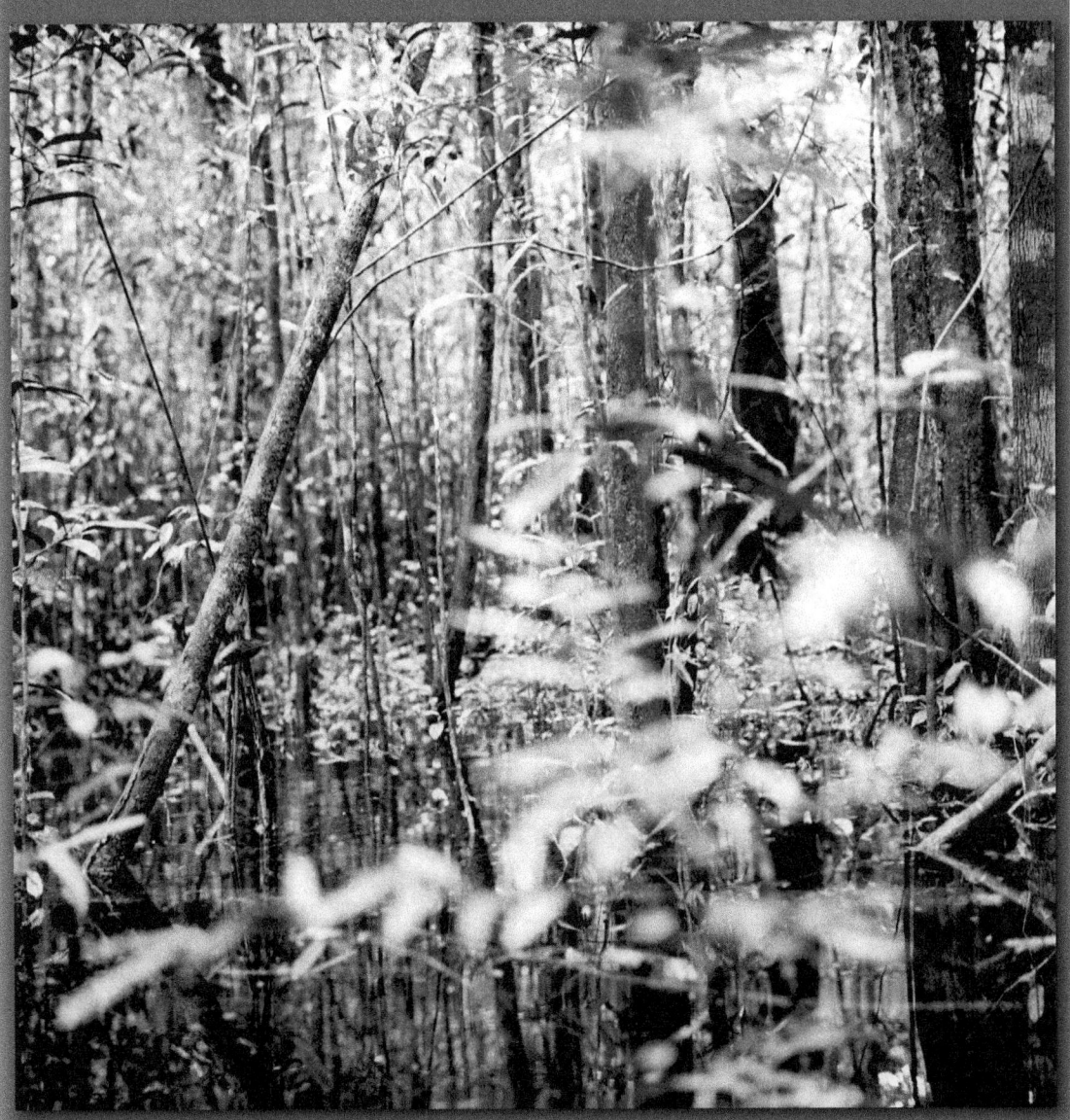

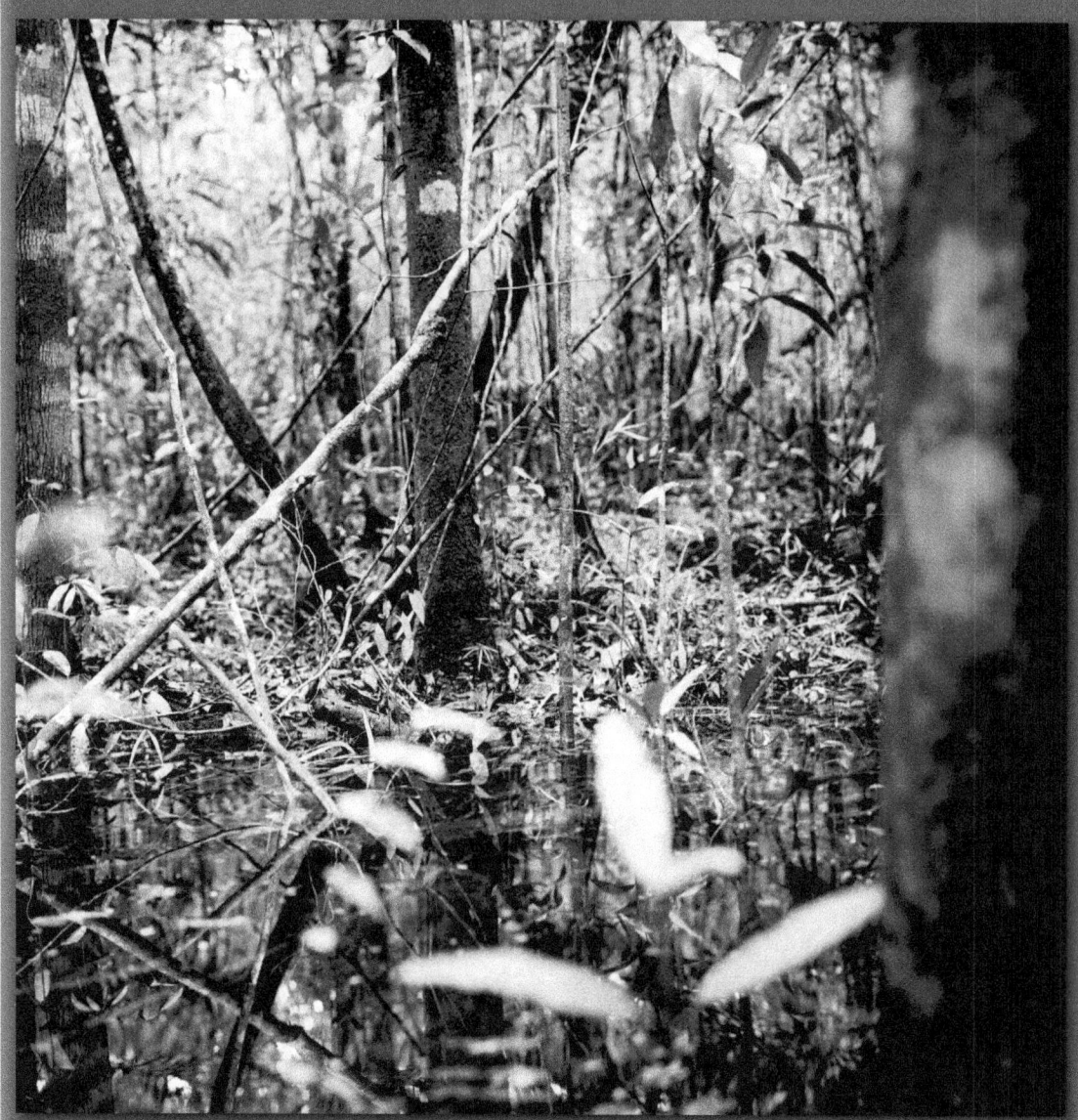

2008

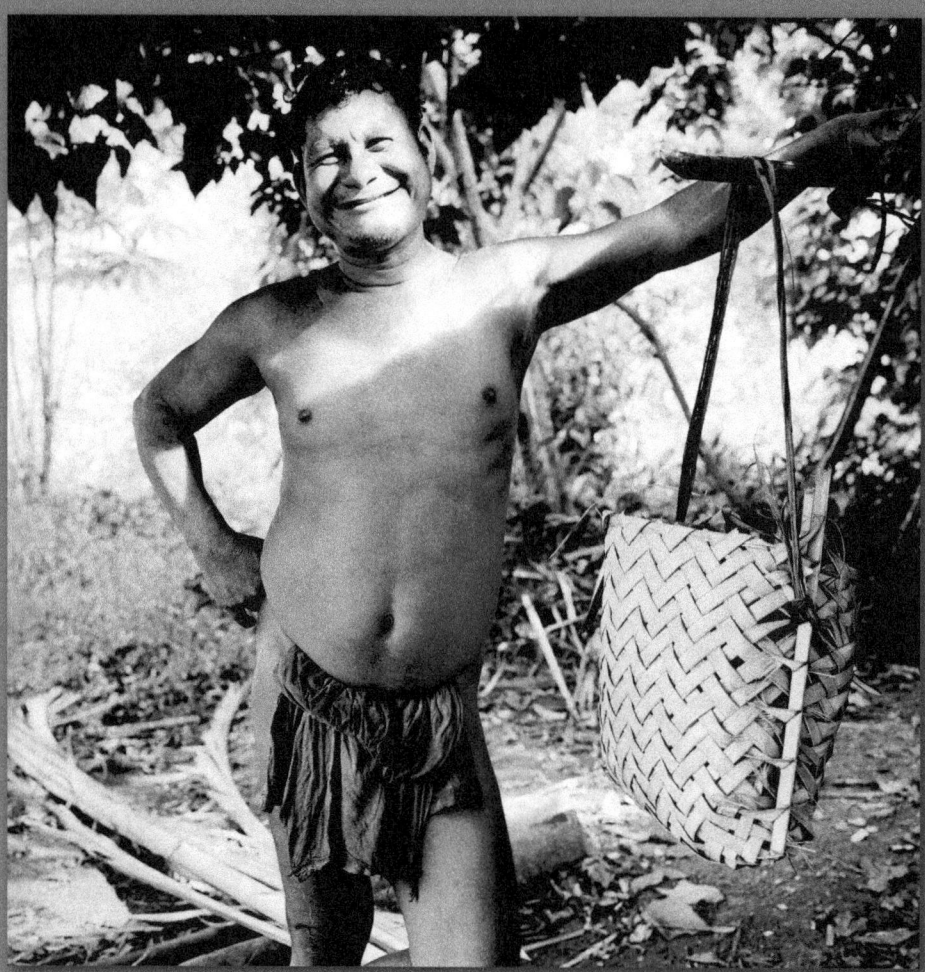

"Edgar" Pirahã in his hut

The original series of 24 images
presented at the catalogue of the

N.M.A.I. exhbition
April 22th - 2008

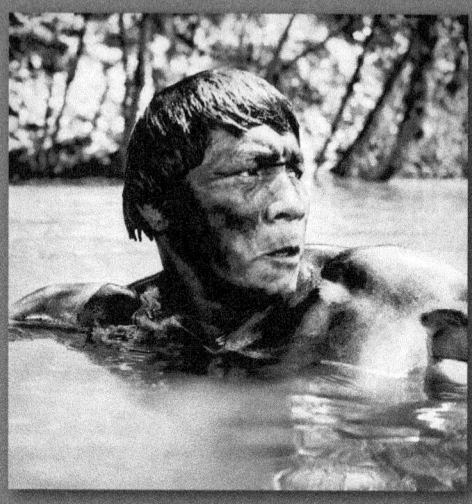
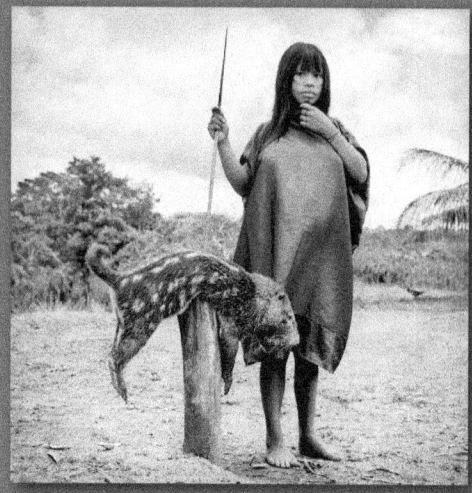
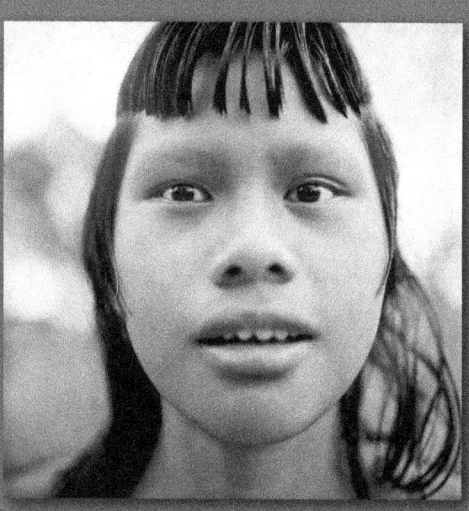
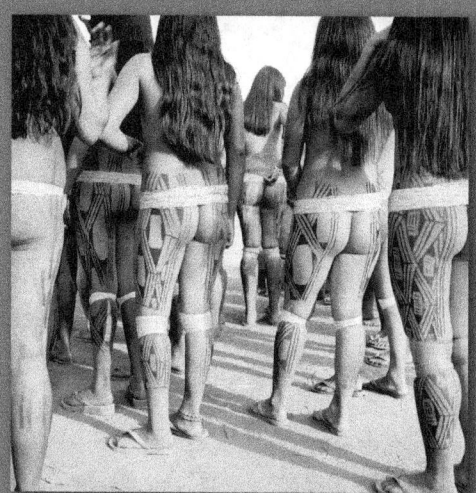

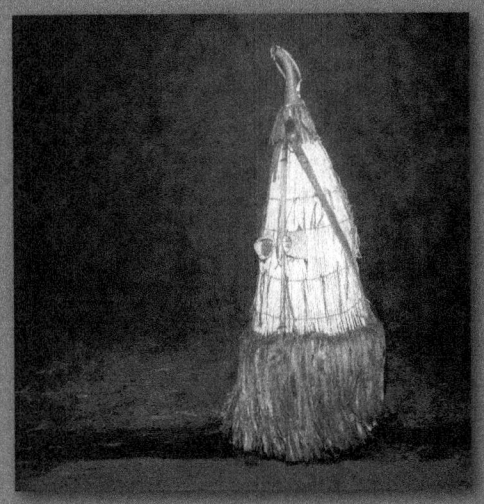
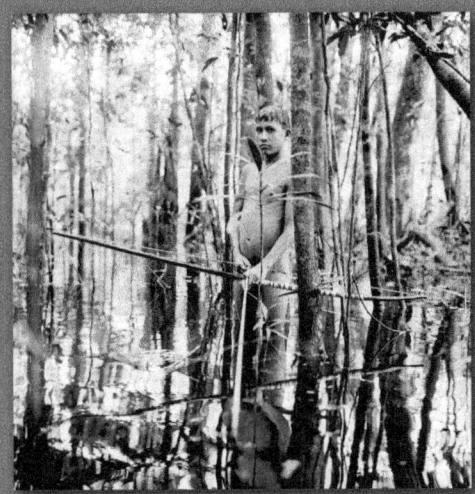
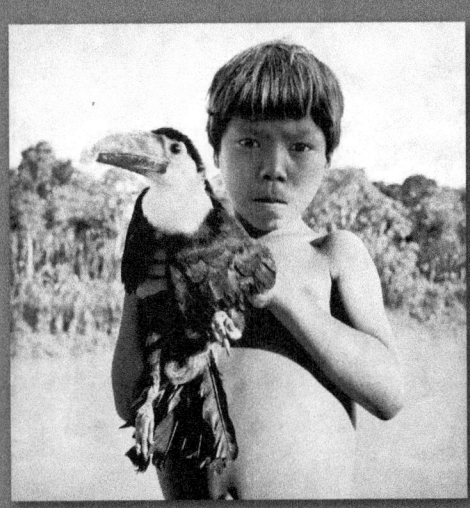
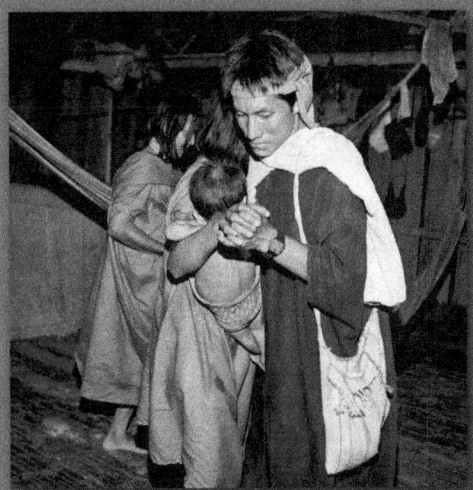

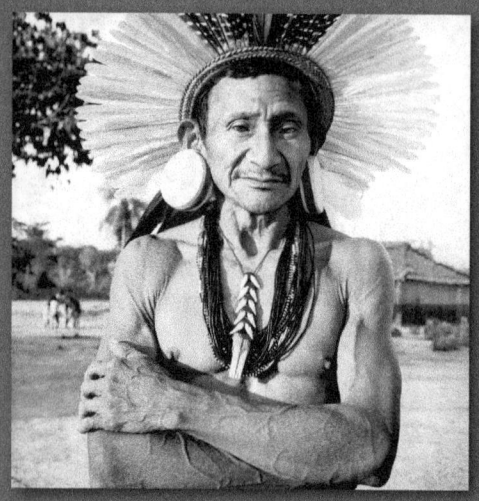
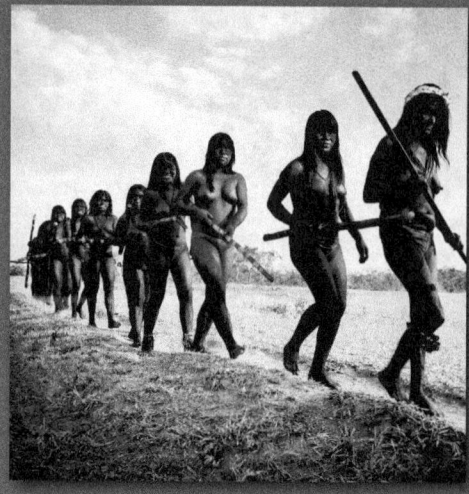
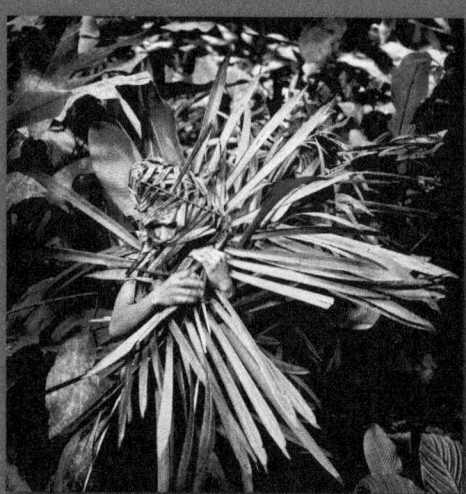
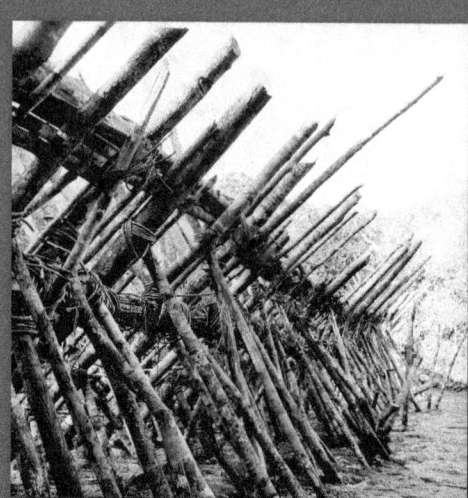

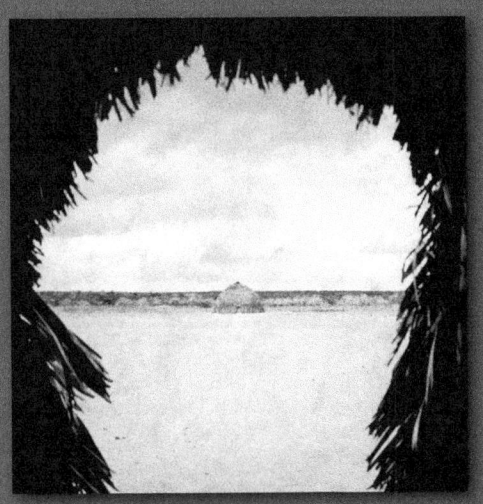
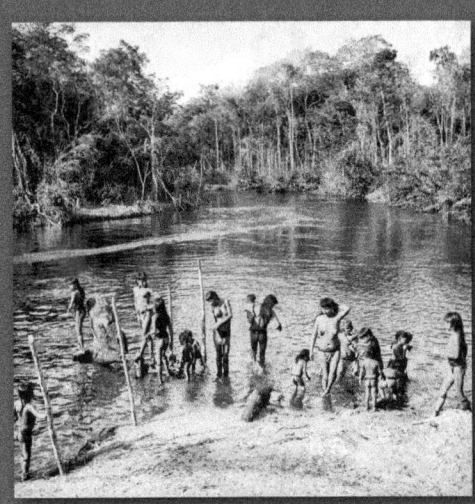
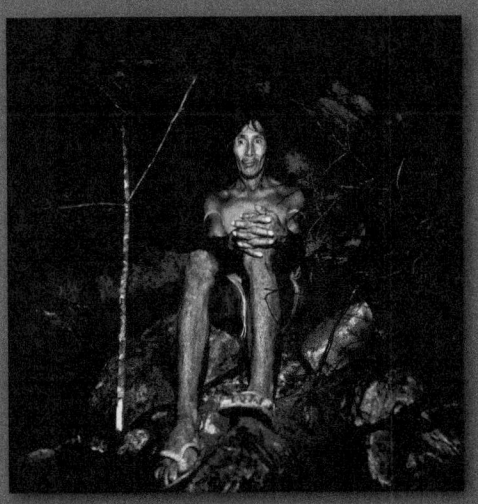
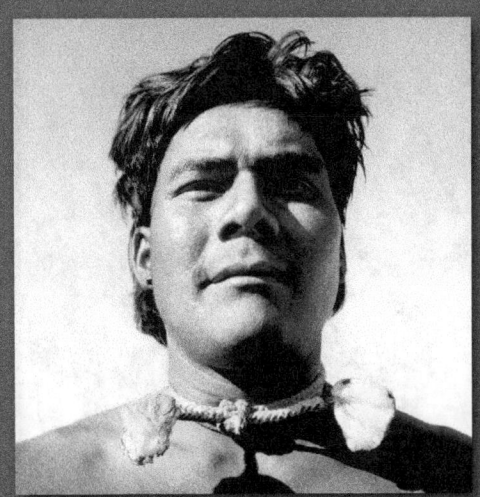

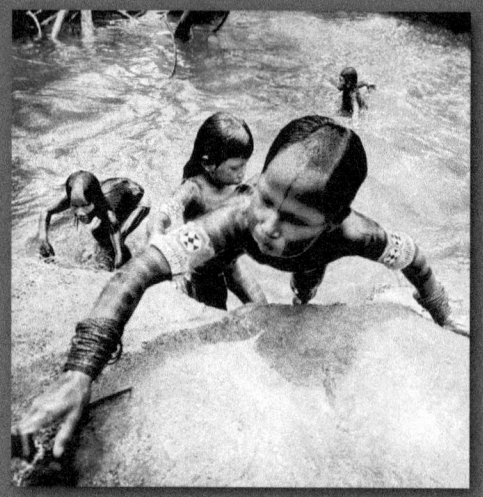
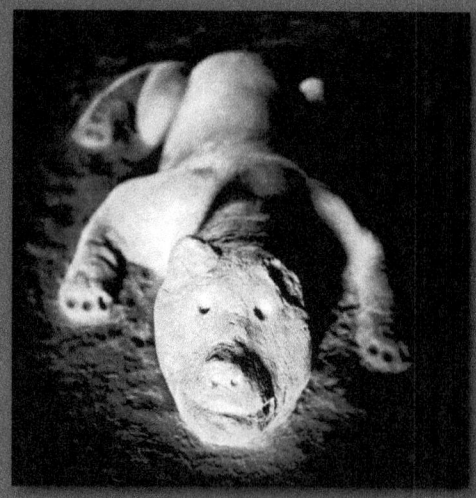
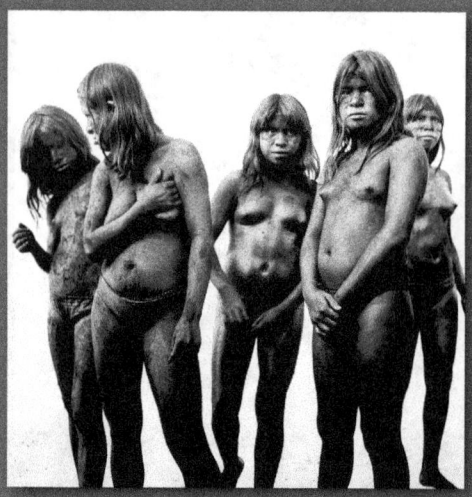
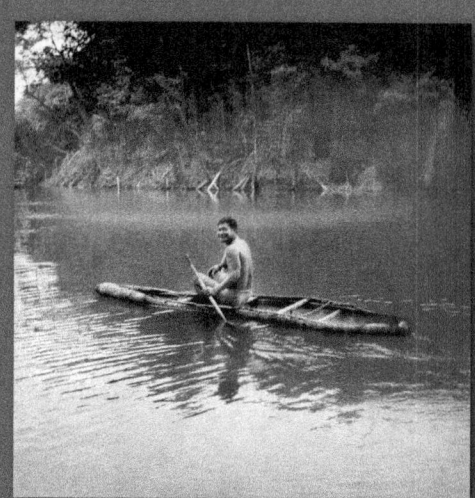

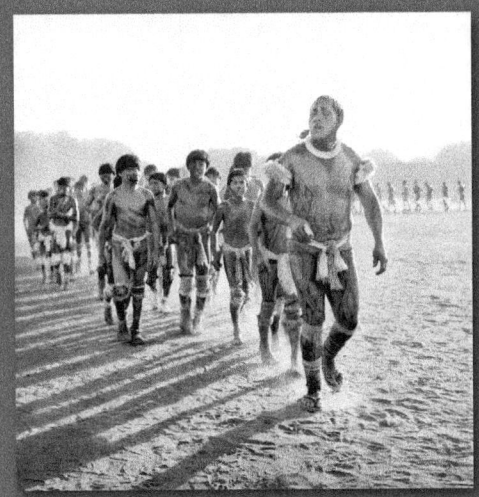

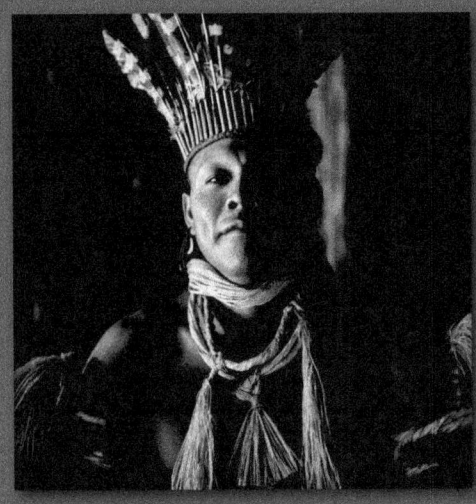

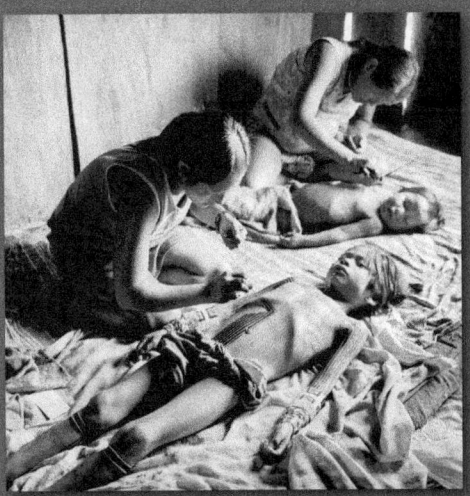

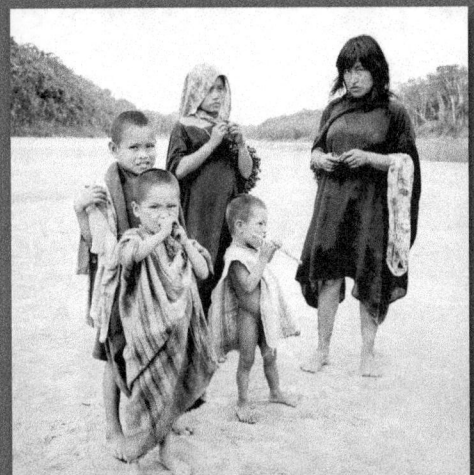